"EE BAH GUM" THE YORKSHIREMAN

A Queen's Guard - Amateur Boxer - Coal Miner

The Story of Arnold Stuart Hinchcliffe

Compiled by the Yorkshireman's Daughter
—
Alison Simpson

Copyright © Alison Simpson 2022
Published by Alison Simpson

Cover by Ina Kuehfuss at *www.inawonderworld.com*
Interior Design by Ina Kuehfuss at *www.inawonderworld.com*
Edited by Leeza Baric at *www.leezabaric.com*
Yorkshireman's Daughter at *www.alisonsimpson.com.au*

All rights reserved. No part of this book may be reproduced by any mechanical photographic, or electronic process, or in the form of a phonographic recording: nor may it be stored in a retrieval system, transmitted, or otherwise be copied for public or private use—other than for "fair use" as brief quotations embodied in articles and reviews—without prior written permission of the publisher.

Cataloguing-in-Publication Data is on file at Legal Deposit State Library of Queensland and the National Library of Australia.

Paperback ISBN: 13:978-0-6454756-0-9
Hardback ISBN: 13:978-0-6454756-1-6
1st Edition, April 2022

Dedicated to my husband, Gary, who continues to support me in all my endeavours, no matter how far off the beaten track I traverse.

CONTENTS

Preamble   9

1.   **Early Life in Yorkshire**   11
Walton (1934), Moorends (1938), Walton (1941)

2.   **A Young Lad in Kent**   19
Deal (1946), Boxing Clubs (1947), First Fights (1948-1949)

3.   **Into the Workforce**   29
Coal Mining (1949), Merchant Navy and First Voyage (1950), The Pit (1951), Deal Boxing Fair (1951)

4.   **Military National Service**   49
Recruit School (1952), 2nd Battalion (1953), Deployment (Canvey Island and Isle of Sheppey)

5.   **Spreading Wings**   65
Falling in Love, Boxing for the Battalion, Deployment (Canal Zone - Egypt), 21st Birthday

6.   **Civvy Street**   83
Deal Pier Labourer, Courting Joan, Back to the Pit, Wedding Day

7.   **Earning a Crust for the Family**   93
Reservist, Coal Miner, Dover Docker, Ferry Waiter, Paul, Army Reserve Duty, John, Alison

8.   **Itchy Feet**   123
Yorkshire (1965), Kent (1968), Yorkshire (1970)

9.   Australia Versus England   139
Emigration to Australia (1972), Ping-Pong Pom (1977), Double Back (1978)

10.   Enforced Early Retirement   161
Spinal surgery (1986), New Life at Shoalhaven Heads (1989), Relocation to Folkestone (1996)

11.   The Travelling Nomads   183
Australia Calls (2000) Invitation to Meet the Queen, Coast to Coast Walk, QE2 World Cruise (2002), Pacific Ocean Back-to-Back Cruising (2004)

12.   Unpacking for Good   205
River Views

Epilogue – Family Reflections   209

PREAMBLE

Arnold Stuart Hinchcliffe was born in Walton, Yorkshire, England on Saturday 10th February 1934

PARENTS:

**Stanley Hinchcliffe (1907 - 1981)
Olga Savina Smales (1915 - 1981)**

"E yup" (hello), welcome to the tales of a Yorkshireman. Make yourself a brew (cup) of Yorkshire tea, sit back and enjoy my dad's wondrous 70 years of living life as a very proud Yorkshireman.

The tales are divided into two parts. Part One has Dad's colourfully recounted memories wrapped up with his Yorkshire accent or expressions. At 66-68 years of age, Dad completed the first 35 years of his autobiography with the help of my brother, Paul. Dad dictated, as Paul typed, reliving all his favourite tales of what it was like growing up as a child during World War II in England, travelling around the world with the Merchant Navy as a young teenager, following on to the Grenadier Guards in the Army and working as a coal miner throughout most of his life. His story is interspersed with his regular family life and his itchy feet, relocating numerous times. I have added clarification to his tales in italics.

Part Two is where I picked up the family pen, piecing together his remaining years to complete his life story. There are snippets of individual member's family stories highlighting the Hinchcliffe characters. This book provides a deeper understanding of our ancestors' lived experiences, often through difficult times. I hope our children and future generations are inspired by the tales of their Yorkshireman forbearer—Arnold Stuart Hinchcliffe and that his story gives them a sense of belonging and understanding of where they came from.

Yorkshire Expressions

ee bah gum (polite swear word)

nowt (nothing)

butty (sandwich)

dinner (lunch)

tea (dinner)

somat (something)

lass (girl)

lad (boy)

faffing (wasting time)

brass (money)

ta (thanks)

tarra (goodbye)

1
EARLY LIFE IN YORKSHIRE

Walton (1934)

I was born in a small mining village called Walton near Wakefield in the county of Yorkshire in England. My father, grandfather and uncles were all coal miners. Walton only had three streets, one pub, one shop and one small school. The school was two miles away. We walked to and from school, as there wasn't any public transport.

My parents were on a miner's wage, so they couldn't afford a car. At that time, no one had a car in the village. As time went on, I recall the midwife had a small car and I suppose the doctor had one too. The local Bobby (Policeman) had a bike, which would be of little use today, chasing criminals. There was a bus service that went to Wakefield, a bigger town. We didn't go there often, but when we did, it was a very big treat.

Our parent's first home was a couple of hundred yards from the Pit (coal mine). The design was commonly known as a "two up-two down" house, which had no toilet. We had to walk 50 yards down the street to the public toilet. It was comparable to what Australians call an outside "Dunny". We lived in that house from 1934 to 1938.

On one occasion, I remember going missing as my mother had to ask the Lorry drivers to look for me. They found me at the bottom of the coal chute, fast asleep. Luckily, at the time, there was no coal coming down the chute. Had there been, then I would not be writing my story today.

Whilst living in Walton, my parents had another son, Douglas. He was born on the 31st of January, 1938. *My dad was very close to Douglas, particularly in early life and then again in their senior years. Their working lives often had them living great distances apart.*

Moorends (1938)

Luckily, coal miners and farmers were exempt from compulsory enlistment into the Army. My father later became a Deputy at the Pit, working at Thorne Colliery near Doncaster. That meant we were upgraded to a Deputy's house in the village of Moorends. This was further away, but much better for our family, as it was safer for children to play. We lived here until 1941. During the war, food was scarce, so we had ration books for buying our groceries.

I was away from school for nine months with rheumatic fever as a young lad. Unable to walk, I spent most of that time in bed. On occasion, the doctor carried me to the window to watch the children playing in the street. Eventually, I got back to school, and it was great to be playing outside with my friends again.

This long episode of rheumatic fever may have contributed to Dad's heart failure later in life because this disease can permanently damage the heart valves. Thankfully, Dad loved his sport and kept fit throughout his life, which may have prolonged his lifespan.

My parents took Douglas and me to the pictures (movie theatre). Before we could leave for the pictures, my father had to dampen the fire, dim the lights, and close the curtains in the house because of the war.

We often went to the pictures on a Saturday afternoon to watch *Flash Gordon*. It was a movie that today would be like *Star Trek*. After the pictures, we would go to a café nearby to buy a glass of lemonade. The picture house was not far from home, so we were able to walk there. We just took walking for granted and that is probably the reason why I've always liked walking.

During our time in Moorends, we had to get under the stairs with our gas masks on during the bombing of a nearby town called Hull. An all-clear signal would let us know when it was ok to get out from under the stairs.

Interestingly, whilst I was living in Moorends, my future wife also moved there from her hometown of Dover, to escape the bombing on the south-eastern coastline of England during World War II. We went to the same school but never actually met until back in Dover, when we were teenagers.

Mum tells me she would never have noticed Dad at school being 19 months younger than him. He was one of the big boys.

Walton (1941)

When I was about seven or eight years old, my parents decided to move back to Walton. Walton village itself was surrounded by fields that we loved to play in as children. We moved into a nice house opposite my grandparent's house. At that time, I had a couple of uncles who were in the Army, and they would tell my brother and me a lot of stories.

We lived in a very small house by today's standards. We did not have a proper bath. My mother would fill up a tin bath for us. Every day when my father came home from work, my mother would fill the bath with hot water because in those days, they did not have showers at the Pit.

I enjoyed living opposite my grandparents. I spent a great deal of time playing with their dog, a cocker spaniel named Jack. I took Jack for walks, and he would follow me, even if I wasn't purposely taking him for a walk. On Tuesdays, I often called in to see my grandmother, as she made lovely teacakes, many of which I took home.

Alison Simpson

I remember the day my sister, Sonia, was born. I was told by the midwife to run to the Pit to tell my father of my sister's birth. I will never forget my father's big grin, and his white teeth gleaming through his blackened face of coal dust. She was born on 25th January 1946. *Dad always had a special place in his heart for his sister.*

During the early part of the war, we had to take gas masks to school just in case we needed them. For our school uniform, we wore short trousers and a cap. When it was cold, we put our hands into our trouser pockets, until someone would shout out that the headmaster was coming down the lane in his car. He was one of the few people who had a car in those days. If we had been seen walking to school with our hands in our pockets, we would get "the cane". The headmaster did not need our parent's consent to punish us. If we nodded off in class, the teacher would throw a wooden duster at us, and he rarely missed.

Walton was a quiet place. As children, we spent a lot of our time playing outside. There was no such entertainment as television, video games or play-stations. When I got older, my parents allowed me to go to Wakefield by bus to buy fish and chips for the family. Many of the village children would also go there on Fridays to collect the fish and chips, being a treat for the end of the week.

As children, we always found something to do. There was no homework. It must have been hard for our parents when we couldn't get outside to play. In those days, we had to find our own entertainment.

I lost even more schooling due to the war, as I had to work on a local farm. It was wonderful being on the farm with the horses. Whenever I got the chance, I would help at the farm and there were times when the farmer let me take the horse and cart down to the field. I always wanted to be a farmer as a young boy.

Not all children were able to work on the farm, so I felt very lucky to be allowed on the farm instead of going to school. Potato picking was one of the jobs that children could easily do on the farm. I found potato picking a fun activity to do, being out in the fields in the fresh air. Whilst I was on my lunch break from potato picking, I decided to climb a tree that was in the middle of the field. I climbed the tree but fell out and hurt myself. The story got back to school that I had hurt myself falling out of the tree, landing 100 feet below. This was not even close to what really happened.

In the winter months, we would make snow skies out of beer barrels by nailing strips of the barrel to our old boots or shoes. If we were lucky, we would use sledges on the snow slopes. Douglas and I never had our own sledge but would share with others.

Christmas time was a good time and I have very happy memories. We would start our Christmas carol singing with most of the children from the village. If we were the first out in the evening, we got some small payment for singing the carols. One house we always tried to head to first was some way from the village. We thought the owners must have had something to do with the Mint as we always were given a new coin for our singing. A big wall surrounded this house. It was always the butler that presented us with the new coins. I expect the owners felt sorry for us, as we were mostly coal miner's children. This house owner had a car too.

We used to sit on the train embankment and record the train numbers. We would sit there for hours. Another pastime was helping on the canal. Barges went up and down carrying all kinds of things. I used to open the lock gates and ride to the next one. The canal is where I learnt to swim. If we could get out of going to Sunday school, that is where we would go. We often had to hide our swimming costumes in the garden beds, then make our way up to the canal.

One Sunday, we had to go into the canal without our swimming costumes. As the water was cold, we stood there in our "Sunday best" and were having second thoughts about jumping in. Who should appear but the girl from across the road. We had no choice but to jump in and hide, as we were not supposed to be there. She was older than us and was taking my sister out in her pram.

When the weather was fine, during the summer months, we played in the fields and in the streams. We would dam a stream up to make it deep enough for jumping in and swimming. As we made the dam walls with mud, we became extremely filthy, so rather than go home dirty and have a tin bath, we would clean off the dirt in the stream. Some Saturday mornings we caught a bus into Wakefield to go swimming in the public baths in Almshouse Lane. It was a rare treat to swim here. We did enjoy ourselves.

School Photograph of Arnold and Douglas.

Alison Simpson

2
A YOUNG LAD IN KENT

Deal (1946)

As the war was coming to an end, my parents decided to move to the south of England. As children, we had not been anywhere other than a week's caravan holiday to Clayton Bay, which was on the East Coast of Yorkshire. The thought of moving to another part of the country sounded good to Douglas and I. Better still, it was a seaside town called Deal in the county of Kent. My father travelled to Deal first so he could get a job before we arrived.

When the war had ended, it was much easier to travel. A lot of servicemen were coming home. We left Walton to travel down to Kent by train with my uncle. Unfortunately, all of us did not get seats, as the train was full of soldiers, so we had to sit on the floor. It took all night by train just to get to London. We arrived in London early the next morning.

One of the first things we noticed about London was the damaged buildings from the bombing. We took a taxi to Buckingham Palace to see the Changing of the Guard. I remember saying to my mother, "I will be a soldier like that one day". I thought they looked so smart in their red uniforms. London streets were full of homeless people, sadly, having nowhere to go after their homes were bombed in the war.

Alison Simpson

It took a few hours on the train from London to Deal. We had no home to go to either. All our possessions were in our suitcases that we had brought from Yorkshire. Having no furniture, we had to start from scratch once we found our new home. Finding a home wasn't easy, as many houses in Deal had been bombed too, being on the coastline of the English Channel.

In the meantime, we moved in with my uncle, being my father's brother. My uncle had a wife and two daughters. They had a lovely home opposite a park. The house had a large garden. Our family found it challenging living with my cousins though, as they seemed very posh. It was the first time we had met them.

We ate our meals in the dining room. This was new to us, as we didn't have such a luxury in Walton. My parents had a lovely house in Walton, but not as big as my uncle's house. Probably just as well, because if it had been big, we would likely never have moved to Kent. Whilst living at my uncle's house, on my first day at school in Deal, I was sent to the wrong school quite embarrassingly.

I'm always grateful to my aunty and uncle for taking my family in because Deal has many fond memories for me. If they had never taken us in after the war, we might not have left Yorkshire. I still have my Yorkshire accent to this day, as many people remind me.

People who live in the south of England rarely travelled north to Yorkshire. It was considered that "up north" was full of factories and coal mines. There were four coal mines in Kent, but most people would not know this as most of the mines were in the countryside away from the towns. We would meet holidaymakers on the beach in Deal and they would be really surprised to hear we had coal mines nearby. There are plenty of stories about Deal locals not liking the coal miners.

We found living in Kent quite difficult at first. To start with, they talked differently to us. It was not too bad for my sister, Sonia, as she was still young, being able to pick up the local southern accent. Living by the sea made up for any negatives, as I loved summer swimming in the ocean.

After school, I often took the next-door-neighbour's racing dogs for a walk up to Kingsdown village. That was about a two-mile walk there and back. Sometimes I would have three dogs with me. I have always loved dogs. I believe this was as a result of my grandparent's cocker spaniel, Jack. I didn't get paid for taking the neighbour's dogs for a walk. The dogs probably only got a walk when I took them. I just picked them up and brought them back, never ever meeting the owners.

It was not long before my mother found us a house to rent in Blenheim Road, near a park. Our three-storey house had no electricity, only gas lamps, nevertheless, we felt luckier than most people. There had been an enormous amount of bombing on that part of the coast, damaging many houses, as we were not far from Dover.

When we moved into our house, being the eldest child, I was hoping to choose my own bedroom. The one I liked overlooked the park. It would have been great for me, as I could see if any of my mates or others were playing football. It was not meant to be. I was very disappointed, because Mum and Dad had a different idea; they took in a lodger. He was an old man, older than my father. This man worked at the Pit with my father. He stayed with my parents for 20 years until he died. Douglas and I had the attic bedrooms on the top floor of the house.

The move to the south coast was good for my parents. We did not have to go to church. Even my parents didn't go anymore. They started "old-time dancing", which they loved. My father would often act about, making fun of the seriousness, while dancing. It would make my mother angry, as she always took dancing so seriously. I can still see the big cheeky grin on my father's face.

I love how this cheeky, mischievous trait has been passed down the Hinchcliffe family line. We have many resemblances of cheekiness with Paul and John, my brothers, who have always loved a good joke or tease. Now my sons often tease me for a laugh.

My parents made me take the children out for walks, so the adults could get some peace and quiet. It was a full and noisy house when we were all home together. Usually, I would only have to take my sister, Sonia, for a walk. Sometimes I took her on very long walks all the way to Kingsdown village. On some occasions, I was also asked to take my cousins for a walk. At times, I would allow my youngest cousin to get into the pushchair (pram) simply to stop her from crying because she didn't want to walk. Being the oldest child, I felt it was my responsibility to keep the children quiet in and out of the house.

One of my regular jobs was to queue for bread at Cavell's Bakery shop during my school break. I did this for my mother and aunty. Bread at the time was still rationed as it was just after the war. I was an Errand Boy, being the oldest child in our family. After delivering the bread to my aunty and back home, I then had to go to school.

Late summer through to autumn, when we were out walking, it was common for us to collect blackberries that were growing wild near Walmer Castle.

Walmer Castle was the residence of many royal and political figures. The Duke of Wellington [1759-1852] lived his later years there, it was one of his favourite homes. He was a highly regarded military man who served twice as the Prime Minister of England. At the age of 83, he died at Walmer Castle.

The Queen's Mother [1900-2002] used to stay in this Castle on her summer holidays in July most years. To commemorate her 95th birthday, Pitt's walled garden was renovated to form The Queen Mother's Garden.

When we moved into the house on Blenheim Road, the first thing I wanted to do was get myself a paper round so that I could buy a push bike. At one time, I had two paper rounds. In those days, paper rounds were restricted to boys. With two rounds, I found it hard to finish them before school. I often finished them off during the school lunch break. That did not last long, as the customers were not pleased about receiving their paper at lunchtime. After saving money over a considerable amount of time, I had enough money to buy a secondhand bike. I loved delivering papers on Sunday morning as I was able to have a sleep in, not starting the round until 8am. I enjoyed the paper round delivering along the Deal seafront. It was not so pleasant in the winter months, though.

I loved seeing my father going for a swim in the sea, having never seen him swim in Yorkshire before. I was surprised at the amount of people that could not swim in Deal, despite living so close to the beach. I was glad that I could swim, having taught myself. My uncle tried to teach me how to swim at the Wakefield Swimming Baths, but I was too frightened. I felt much safer learning to swim in the canals with my friends.

In Deal, we started swimming around Easter time. The water was usually cold, but as youngsters, we tried to be the first to go into the sea. The council would start putting out the deck chairs and the tents for changing rooms. When it rained, we put our clothes under the deck chairs. As you were supposed to hire the deck chairs, sometimes one of us would hire a single chair and we would all share it. We found living in Deal at the seaside was great for everyone.

We would swim out to a shipwreck that was 400 yards off Deal beach, going around it and back to shore. Due to the danger of strong tides that could drag us off course, we were careful to walk up the beach, well past the wreck before swimming out. The shipwreck was a popular haunt for us young lads.

The wreck was an American liberty ship, SS James Harrod, carrying jeeps and jerry cans full of petrol bound for Antwerp in Belgium at the end of World War II. As it travelled along the coast at night, it collided into an anchored liberty ship, Raymond B Stevens, which was carrying ammunition bound for Europe. Sadly, four young crew members of the SS James Harrod died, but the rest were saved by jumping into lifeboats and the final crew, including the captain, were rescued by a Dutch rescue vessel, Tromp.

I found school in Deal hard to begin with, but soon made lots of new friends. One friend who had also moved down to Deal from Yorkshire was Jimmy Ainscough. My deep friendship with Jimmy continued forever. We ran into each other many times throughout our lives.

Jimmy came from Yorkshire, not far from where my family had lived. His father had been a coal miner too. We both had the same broad Yorkshire accent, were in the same class at school and had similar backgrounds. We felt like brothers, having a great understanding of each other from the first time we met. *Thinking of Jimmy now, he was a bit of a larrikin, often joking around. Maybe it's also a Yorkshire trait.*

Jimmy and I knocked about together after school. As children, we would go all over the place to play. One of our favourite places was The Glen. It was close to Walmer Castle, a long way from where we both lived. We both joined the Youth Club, where we played table tennis. Later, I joined the Boys Brigade only because they went to the Marines Swimming Baths. The indoor baths were good in the winter months.

In 1992, I met Jimmy at his shop, Pandora's Box in Folkestone. I walked into his shop and announced I was Arnold Hinchcliffe's daughter. His big smile and fists up for a boxing match said it all. He told me with a stern grin that he had many tall tales about Dad, and they were not going to be disclosed to anyone. At least we got a photo together and Dad was pleased that I had met him, his best mate.

Boxing Clubs (1947)

Jimmy and I decided to join the Walmer Boxing Club. Bill Davis, from the Pit, had started the Boxing Club. There were not many boxers. Jimmy and I were two of the youngest boys there. The training was held at the Fire Station in Walmer. Most of the older boys were coal miners. It was not long before a club was formed in Deal. It was a bigger club and used the Drill Hall, which was just 100 yards from where I lived.

As the new club was able to get sponsors, we had better trainers. One of whom was Neal McCain. He had been the second-best Welter-Weight Boxer in England, an ex-professional boxer. As they were good trainers, they would not allow any nonsense. We would have to work hard. We started with loosening up exercises, then three rounds of shadow boxing, followed by three rounds of hitting the punch bag. To quicken us up, we would go on the punch balls, then a few rounds sparring with someone. To finish up, we would do a few more exercises.

We trained three times a week and were not allowed to be late, or we'd be told off. Sometimes I would be late because I listened to a radio thriller serial called *Dick Barton - Special Agent*. This program started in 1946 ending in 1951. Then I would speedily run down to Drill Hall. I was about 13-years-old when I first joined the Boxing Club.

The serial followed the adventures of ex-Commando Captain Richard Barton MC (Noel Johnson, later Duncan Carse and Gordon Davies) who, with his mates Jock Anderson (Alex McCrindle) and Snowy White (John Mann), solved all sorts of crimes, escaped from dangerous situations, and saved the nation from disaster time and again. (https://en.wikipedia.org/wiki/Dick_Barton)

First Fights (1948-1949)

I did not have my first fight until I was 14-years-old. I had a few fights around the local towns such as Ramsgate and Sandwich. I was later entered into the Kent Championships. These were always held in Maidstone. The first year I entered, I won the Kent Championships for my age. That meant I had to go on to represent Kent in the Southern Counties Championships. I won that title, so I then became the Southern Counties Champion. I won this again in my second year. If I had won my next fight against the Western Counties, I would have gone on to the finals at Albert Hall in London. The last boy I boxed went on to win the England Championships. I was unlucky to have met such talented boys so early in the Championships.

Jim Wicks approached me to become a professional boxer. I didn't think I could make a good living out of boxing, so I didn't take up the offer. I never took my boxing seriously. One time, I even had to borrow some boxing boots. Jim Wicks later became Henry Coopers' manager. Henry Cooper became the British Heavyweight Champion 1959 to 1969 and 1970 to 1971. Also, the European Heavyweight Champion 1964, 1968 to 1969.

I played for the school football team most Saturday mornings. It was a great team, with several of the boys going on to play for some top clubs. I took a lot of interest in athletics, which I was pretty good at. I didn't enjoy cricket, so when cricket was on, I would train by running around the track.

I joined the Betteshanger Athletic Club. It was a good club. The officials took a lot of interest in me and tried to talk me into giving up swimming to focus on athletics. I raced in Maidstone, where several runners were competing for the upcoming Olympics in 1952. I was only entered into the race for experience, subsequently I came last.

One afternoon when Jimmy and I were dawdling back to school, realising we were going to be late, we both started to worry. We were frightened of our teacher. If we fronted up late, we would both get the cane. We decided to play truant to avoid the caning and headed off to the marshes for the rest of the day. It didn't help. We both got the cane the next day at school.

Another morning, walking to school with my brother, Douglas, the truant officer, stopped us. He told me to make sure my brother got to school on time. I didn't have the nerve to tell him that I, too, should also be getting to school. He must have thought I looked too old for school.

The Education Act of 1944 succeeded in extending the compulsory education age from 14 to 15. This became effective from 1947, after World War II. However, my school was not prepared for this, even in 1949, my final year of school. No lessons were arranged for the entire year. I recall the classrooms we used in that last year were old sheds that needed pulling down. It was at the back of one of those old sheds that I had my first and last cigarette.

Arnold on his bike in South Street, Deal.

Alison Simpson

3
INTO THE WORKFORCE

Coal Mining (1949)

There wasn't much work to choose from in Deal. It was more of a holiday destination or retirement area. Many of my schoolmates joined the Royal Marines, but I was not ready for something like that. It was accepted that as I came from a mining family, I would become a coal miner, too. The sons of coal miners did not leave school with a good education, as so much schooling was missed during the war.

I left school on Friday to start work on the following Monday in the coal mine, Betteshanger Colliery. I was to catch the 5.30am bus to the Pit. Unfortunately, on my first day, I caught the wrong bus, ending up at a different Pit, Tilmanstone. I had to walk back to Betteshanger Colliery, which was about three miles. This was not a good start, but no one seemed to mind too much.

The first 15 weeks of my training were on the Pit top. We were not allowed to go down the Pit full time until after this training period. During training, we had several days down the Pit each week to acclimatise us to the underground environment, as well as first aid training. The 15 weeks seemed a long time for me. I would have only been about 15 and a half years old when I was finally allowed to go down the Pit full time.

My first job down the Pit was to work on haulage. This meant I had to couple up coal tubs together before they were raised to the surface. The coal left the coal face on a conveyor belt, arriving at a loading point to then be dropped down a steel chute into tubs. These tubs would then travel along to a point where I would have to couple them together. The coupled tubs then headed to the Pit bottom on a steel rope to a cage. This cage took the coal to the surface. It was not a good job, but just like any job, you must start somewhere.

I liked the money, although it was not a lot by today's standards. When I found out that I was able to do some overtime and by doing so would lift my wages, I started doing double shifts. This meant I was down the Pit for 16 hours. It was a long day for a 15-year-old. Some weeks, I would do three double shifts a week.

During the first few weeks, I handed my entire wage over to my mother. I soon found out from my mates how much they paid their mothers for board. I then had to agree with my mother that I would just pay board each week. As I didn't enjoy shift work, I only stayed working at the Pit for one year. I found that in the winter months it was too cold down the Pit and during the summer months the afternoon shift was frustrating, as I would have preferred to be going to the beach.

At that time, boys were leaving the Pit to join the Merchant Navy. It seemed a great opportunity to do the same. The idea of getting paid while you see the world was very appealing to me. My mother didn't want me to join the Merchant Navy, but she knew I was not happy at the Pit.

Merchant Navy (1950)

After some discussion with my dad, he gave his permission for me to join the Merchant Navy. I could have gone to the moon and my father would still not have minded. He had such an easy-going nature, always having a grin on his face. Mum reluctantly followed suit. I was 16-years-old and still not shaving. The Pit manager was not happy when I gave him my notice to resign. I can understand his disappointment, as the Coal Board had given 15 weeks of training and I only stayed one year.

I made my own way to the training ship. It was an old sailing ship called the *Vindicatric*. It was docked at a place called Sharpness in Gloucestershire. I caught three trains to get there. Being winter, darkness fell quickly. It was the first time that I had been away from home. I only had a few belongings in a small suitcase as I was to get a uniform to wear upon arrival for duty.

Arriving at the docks, it was a Monday night. On Monday nights, they always had a boxing match in the Seaman's Mission. There was a boxer who was winning every week, being paid 10 shillings for each win. Ten shillings were a lot of money for anyone who did not have a job.

I was prepared to have a go at boxing myself and boxed this boy who had been winning each week. I managed to beat him, and I was paid the 10 shilling purse. After that fight and for the next six weeks, I could not go wrong at the camp. Being a good boxer was highly regarded in those days.

We were not paid any wage during training. Instead, they used our unemployment money to look after us. Any money the trainees had usually was sent by their parents. The 10 shillings I made from boxing on the first night came in handy.

The food was bad. We would often see a lot of cockroaches on the ship. Most parents would send food parcels, which was always very well received. At night we went down to the Seaman's Mission where we would get cups of tea and buy a cake. Sometimes we would buy a fruit loaf and a packet of butter, which was cheaper than buying a few cakes.

We were up at the crack of dawn, no later than 6am. We never got a second call. Snow was on the ground at that time, and we would have to run 50 yards to get a shower. There weren't many showers, so we didn't hang around too long, as there was always a long queue.

After six weeks of training, we were ready to be Saloon Boys on the Liner. At that stage, we were not old enough to be on the Liner. I had never given it a thought as to what my job was going to be. All I could think about was that I would be getting paid to see the world. I had met some of the boys who had come home on leave from this job. They always seemed to have a lot of money to spend. For a 16-year-old, the job came second to the thought of earning all that money.

On completion of the training, I was given a railway warrant (free pass) to go home until I was required to report to my first posting. This was to be on a ship called *The Warwick Castle*. It was from the Union Castle Line. This company was not considered good, but it was a job, and I was to see the world. I only had one week spare from the time I finished training to when I was to report to the ship. I stayed the Sunday night at the Seaman's Mission near Tilbury Docks before joining the ship on Monday morning.

I was going to be away for 10 weeks. We were heading to South Africa with the first stop at Gibraltar. We were expecting rough seas for five days through the Bay of Biscay. My job was to look after the officers, making their beds and keeping their cabins clean. I was also required to serve them all their meals in the First-Class Lounge. It was certainly a different life than being a coal miner. The Officers' cabins were on the top deck of the ship.

For the first five days, I was seasick but still had to work very hard. Serving food when you cannot face the food yourself was not fun. One time I thought I would save time by throwing the rubbish over the side of the ship. It was early in the morning, being very dark and quiet, no one was about except for a few Officers who were on duty (and it was their cabins that I was cleaning) so I did not worry about it. However, I had not counted on the wind blowing it all back into my face. It was the last time I did that.

Gibraltar

Arriving in Gibraltar, I was really looking forward to my first port of call, only to find out that the ship was to stay half a day to take on supplies. I soon realised most passenger carrying ships only stopped to pick up passengers or for supplies. That was to be my first disappointment.

I should have realised that, like myself, passengers must be fed every day. This meant a 10 week trip was 10 weeks without a day off. If we were lucky to be in port for a whole day, I would still have to be on board for each meal service. I needed to be smartly dressed always, while in the First-Class dining room serving the Officers. At least I got to see the Rock of Gibraltar from the ship's deck.

The Merchant Navy was certainly not what I thought it would be. I found it was hard work with very little time off. I was always late to bed and early to rise for my shifts. It was not long before I discovered I had no free time to spend my earnings. There was a room on the ship where the older crew would go to have a drink and a smoke. Being only 16-years-old, I did not drink or smoke, so I would only be able to buy a Pepsi Cola. If I was lucky, the ship would stay in port long enough for me to go ashore. I used part of my wages to buy presents for my mother and sister. At that time, I did not get such things as tips, because the officers only gave a tip at the end of the voyage.

Genoa, Italy

After leaving Gibraltar, the next port of call was Genoa in Italy. It was good going through the Mediterranean as the sea was calm, much different from the Bay of Biscay. During time off, we were allowed to use a small, secluded area to sit and sunbath.

It was in Genoa that the first problems started. We had left London short of crew and it came to a head in Genoa. The head waiter confronted the Captain over the issue and as a result, more crew were flown out from London. They promised that we would have more crew to join the ship at the next port of call. They only did this to keep the ship moving. We had a couple of days in Genoa, but there was not a lot for me to see. I only wandered around the town. The older crew would go into the bars.

Port Said, Egypt

Our next port of call was Port Said. That sounded good to me, as it was a very different kind of culture. When we arrived in Port Said, it was just like Gibraltar. We anchored away from the quay, so I was not able to get ashore.

From the ship, Port Said looked very different from any other port we had been to so far. We did not stay at Port Said for long. Small boats would come alongside our ship to sell their goods. These were mostly small carpets and other small items that they would throw up to the ship so that you could look at them. I did not buy anything, as it was all new to me.

I returned to Port Said three years later, as a soldier in active service. I would never have given it a thought at 16 years of age to go back there again.

Suez Canal, Egypt

We travelled along the Suez Canal in convoy, as it was only wide enough to go one way. It seemed strange having land close on both sides of the ship. We passed many villages along the way. The canal was nicknamed "The Sweet Water Canal" but it was filthy. All sorts of things were thrown into the canal. There was a road that ran alongside the full length of the canal.

Aden, Yemen

Our next port of call was Aden. We never went ashore, but I managed to buy a cigarette lighter in the shape of a camera. I do not know why

I bought it because I did not smoke. I suppose I thought that I must buy something, otherwise I would have got back to London without having bought anything.

In fact, I didn't spend much money at all, as it meant always getting an advance on my wages. I doubt if I knew what wages that I was being paid. I just wanted to see the world, but I didn't see much from the ship's deck.

It was in Aden that one of the deck's crewman bought a monkey onboard. I don't know how he did it, but I recall that the passengers were not impressed. It would run all over the deck. The deck crewman would have gotten into trouble over that. It was funny at the time, but he may not get a job on this ship again after this incident.

Port of Sudan, Sudan

Sudan was our next port of call. Again, we didn't get off the ship. In the three weeks, we only had two days off the ship. I found that after such a long time on the ship it was very strange to walk on land. You felt as though you were still rolling along on a ship.

The head waiter decided to have me serving the passengers. I don't know what happened to serving the Officers, but I still had to clean their cabins. What could I do at 16 years of age? I could not mutiny by myself? I was not old enough to do a waiter's job and was underpaid, not being paid a waiter's wage. I never complained and other waiters never got on to me about it.

The First-Class dining room was called the saloon. I am sure if they had plenty of waiters a new starter like myself would not be allowed to serve the First-Class passengers. When I first started serving the Officers, I am sure they were patient with me, but now it was different because I was serving paying passengers. They were not as friendly towards me; they didn't know my story. They didn't know I should not have been doing this job. It was very disappointing that I was not getting rightfully paid for my work as a waiter either.

This job was hard work with long hours. I had 16 passengers to serve and memorise everyone's orders, as I wasn't allowed to take notes. I carried six plates at a time and found it difficult, particularly when passengers asked for cheeses that I'd never heard of before. I made many mistakes, considering there were 50 or 60 different types of cheese. It was tough for me, so I didn't get many tips.

Being a waiter, I was now going to be serving passengers for the next seven weeks. I accepted that, but I worried if I would deliver the wrong dishes to the wrong passengers. The older waiters gave me little bits of encouragement, but they could not spend too much time with me as they had their own passengers to look after. They did help me out with the cheese selections. The passengers would have a new big menu each day to select from. I'm sure I would have found it much easier if they didn't change the menu.

The evening meal was always late. After the meal, you could either reset your tables before you went back to your cabin or leave them until the next day by getting up extra early before breakfast. I always set my tables before I went back to my cabin. Most of the older waiters would sit about in the mess and drink beer in the evenings after the dinner service. There was not much for me to do in the cabins. The cabins were at the bottom of the ship. I shared my cabin with seven other workers. It was strange at first because the training ship quarters felt like military barracks.

Mombasa, Kenya

Our next port of call was Mombasa on the eastern coast of Africa. It was not much of a place; it had only one main street. The one thing I do remember about Mombasa was they had a bad shoe shop, the same name as a shoe shop in Deal, called Bata. Like most of the ports, we did not stay very long. This was our third time on shore in over three weeks, but it was only for a few hours because passengers had to be served their meals. Several passengers, well-off English people who lived in that part of the world, disembarked there.

Zanzibar, Tanzania

Just a little further down the east coast of Africa was our next port, Zanzibar. It was an island and sounded good, but we were not there long enough. That place would have been quite an adventure for a 16-year-old boy who wanted to see the world to disembark there. We anchored offshore and I could only look from the deck. We threw coins into the sea and watched the young lads that had swum out to the ship dive down to pick up the coins. They would surface with the coins in their mouths. The town of Zanzibar would have been a great place to visit.

Durban and East London, South Africa

We continued down the east coast of Africa, stopping at East London then on to Durban. In Durban, the crew problem arose again. The Captain and head waiter thought the problems were resolved, but this was when the real trouble started. I soon found out what disputes can mean and unfortunately, I was the main reason for the dispute.

To my knowledge, it was to do with my wages. Not that I had received wages, just a few tips along the way. I felt I wasn't cut out to be a waiter, as the passengers disappeared at the end of their trips. I thought perhaps a seaman would have been a better job, but I didn't know how I would have managed scrubbing the decks. Up until then, I hadn't given much thought to my wages. If anyone had asked me what wage I received, I wouldn't have been able to tell them, but I soon learnt. I discovered my wage was well below that of all other waiters, even though they might have had more experience.

Durban, South Africa

We disembarked in Durban. It was a lovely place, being a very modern town with lots of skyscrapers. It was the first time I saw a skyscraper. I originally thought we would only be there for a few days, but it turned out to be over a week, due to the dispute.

The catering crew did not forget about the issue of being short of crew. Doing extra work, they wanted extra money. The passengers were not giving good tips. When we arrived in Durban, the Captain started having meetings. The meetings didn't help, so all the catering crew walked off the ship. I was part of the reason for this dispute. This was my first experience of what could happen when a dispute unfolded.

The National Union of Seaman came in to rectify the situation. It was common knowledge that the National Union of Seaman were inclined to support the company rather than the workers. The Union wanted us to continue working. The Captain asked the seamen to move the ship away from the quayside, but they would not. If the ship was tied up, the company would have to pay big port charges.

We ended up sleeping on the beach or some were lucky and slept at the Seaman's Mission. We spent a lot of time on the beach. In Durban, I enjoyed my first taste of drinking tea in cafés. Each table had a miniature jukebox. As far as the strike was concerned, it didn't bother me, as I didn't have anything to spend my money on. I never gave it another thought.

Being on strike by walking off the ship was classified as being on mutiny. I really thought that mutinies only happened in Admiral Lord Nelson's days in the 18th century. It made all the newspapers in South Africa. Different reporters from a few newspapers interviewed me. I never complained about my wages, but the waiters made me out to be the big reason for the strike. On one occasion, they lifted me up off the ground and cheered me on the quayside. That made the front pages the following day.

Spending time in South Africa, I started to learn about their society and culture. Dark-skinned Africans had to get off the pavement when a white-skinned African walked towards them. They had to step into the gutter. On buses, they had to either sit at the front or the back of the bus. Each bus would have two doors, one for white people and one for dark people.

I made friends with a white South African from a well-off family. His family owned a big, sweet factory. He was going to work his passage to London. That was one way of taking on extra crew. He was much less experienced than I. We became the best of friends, as he was the same age as me.

I managed to get my old job back that I had started with. I looked after the Officers, serving them in the First-Class saloon. I don't know who looked after them while I was in the other saloon, serving the paying passengers. I did not mind, as I only had a few Officers to serve compared to 16 passengers, so I found it much easier.

Cape Town, South Africa

After our short time at sea, the next stop was Cape Town. Cape Town was not as good as Durban, but the Tabletop Mountain was very impressive from a distance. Unfortunately, I didn't get the chance to visit the Tabletop Mountain. I did enjoy walking around the shops in Cape Town, though, but lost track of time and nearly missed the ship's boarding. I got back just in time to start serving the Officers before the ship set sail to the next port.

Saint Helena Island, Atlantic Ocean

The next port of call was St Helena, which is an island in the middle of the Atlantic Ocean, owned by the British Crown. The island is a volcanic rock sticking out of the ocean. Napoleon Bonaparte was exiled there in 1815 and I found that interesting at the time. The reason for calling in there was to deliver supplies from Cape Town to the few people who lived on the island.

We managed to go ashore for a few hours while the ship was tied up in the bay. This island was like Norfolk Island (that I visited much later in life). Supplies were delivered by lunch, so if you missed that, it was a big swim back to the ship. There was an earthquake a few years later, on the island. People were moved back to England but wanted to return when everything had settled down.

Alison Simpson

Las Palmas, Canary Islands, Spain

Our last port of call was into Las Palmas before heading home to London. We had one week to go before we found out if we had been reported for our weeklong mutiny by failing to report for duty in Durban. We all knew if it was reported, we would never get a job back at sea again. If I lost my Merchant Navy job, I would have to go back to the Pit for work. The crossing of the Bay of Biscay was much easier for me this time. I did not get seasick and felt I had developed good sea legs.

Arriving in London, we all got the sack. It was not a good start for a 16-year-old boy. It was my second job in 18 months since I had been out of school. The Union Castle Shipping Company would have lost money because of the strike as the ship arrived in London a week late. If they had left London with a full complement of crew in the first place, the outcome would have been completely different. It was not a good company to work for.

When I arrived home, my mother was quite upset that I had lost my job. She wrote to the company to see if they would take me back. After a few weeks, they responded saying they would take me back. I joined a different ship with the same company a week before it was due to sail to South Africa. Most crews do not join the ship until a few days before the ship sails.

The head waiter and the chief steward gave me all the worst jobs they could find, specifically scrubbing floors. I was sure they wanted to take some revenge on me for getting my job back. It was unlikely they would have known my full story regarding the strike as they had only been on the ship a short time, but things came to a head one night.

I was given a scrubbing job, doing the stairs outside the First-Class Saloon. I just left the bucket and scrubbing brush, collected my belongings, and walked off the ship. It was so late I had to stay in Charing Cross Railway Station until the next day for a train back to Deal. There was no way I would go back to sea. That was the end of my Merchant Navy career.

The Pit (1951)

As things now stood, it would be the Pit, if they would take me back. I really hoped to get my job back. With my father working there and the fact that I had done a year's training, I felt I had a good chance.

As I had only been away from the Pit for less than a year, I was able to get my job back. They sent me to work with the fitters, not far from the coalface. In those days, the coalface workers only got paid for the coal they produced. That could be difficult when the conditions were very rough, which was often the case.

Already the Betteshanger Pit was noted as one of the most militant Pits in England. It certainly had a strong union. The coalface workers received the highest wages in England, but they also had the worst conditions to work in.

I enjoyed working with the fitters; they were older than me. My main job was to go to the coalface to grease and oil the face ends and the main gates. I often stayed on the coalface to help the colliers shovel the coal onto the conveyor. I came off the face looking very black and dirty.

By rights, I was too young to go on the face when the machine was operating. I would go into the main headings of my father's coalface, where he was in charge as the Deputy. These colliers were classed as the big hitters of the Pit as they received the biggest wages in the Pit. At the end of each week, they would give me a few shilling tips. Usually, it was on a Friday.

One Friday, I went up to see the Manager about my wage. If your wages were not right, that was the day you would go to see the Manager. This day the Union was there, and they said as a joke that they were waiting for the day that I would be up there because my father had not paid me the correct wage.

The reasons why there were plenty of problems with the wages was because there were no computers to accurately keep records. My Uncle Sid worked in the Time Office at the Pit. They calculated the wages for at least 700 men who worked at the Pit, with their various roles and different shifts. Most men in the Time Office only worked day shift, so mistakes were easily made.

In those days, the face workers worked with a pick and shovel to get coal. They had air drills to get the coal down, then shovelled the coal onto a conveyor belt, which was really hard work.

Later, when I did my coalface training, I did the same kind of work. It was a few years before a different type of machine came into the Pit. We used wooden props to hold the roof up. Any big jobs the fitters had would have to be done on weekends. I was allowed to come in, and I really enjoyed working with them. Now that I was only paying board, I had more money. I started to go out with some of the lads from the Pit.

Each day upon arrival at the Pit you would pick up your small triangle shaped brass disc called a Check or Motty. It was a little bigger than a 20-cent coin having your personal number on it. Then you proceeded on to the lockers to get changed. I got the same locker I had before I left the Pit earlier. The men I had met before, I met again, which was good.

After leaving the dirty lockers, we collected our lamps from the lamp room. Here we left our brass disc to then pick up a second disc to ensure payment for our shift. This one was not made of brass and would be kept on us until we got off the cage at the pit bottom. The banksman (who operated the signals in and out of the pit cages) then collected this disc, keeping it until you came out of the Pit top cage at the end of the shift. You would only leave early if you had been working in water. The discs were a safety mechanism that you had exited the Pit. No check disc meant you were still down the Pit and they would send in a safety team to find you.

Only one person from each family was allowed to travel up or down in the Pit cages. This was to ensure only one family member succumbing to danger at any one time, should a tragedy occur.

There were plenty of old workings at the Betteshanger coal mine. This mine was first sunk in 1927. There was a small shop near the Pit gate run by a man called Jones. All he sold was cups of tea and cigarettes. It was common for the miners to have one cigarette and a cup of tea when they finished their shift. Sometimes I would meet my father there. He liked a smoke and a cup of tea at the end of his shifts. I didn't go there often though, as I preferred to get home at the end of the shift. By then, I had bought myself a bike, so I didn't have to wait for the bus. It was about three or four miles home.

After working with the fitters for about a year, they gave me a new job working in development. It consisted of three shifts: mornings, afternoons, and nights. It was a big job but less money for me as there was no overtime.

I so much wanted to get my face training done so I could earn more money. I could see that it was going to be a long time before I would be allowed to start my face training. Face training took about 120 days. You were required to complete the full course before you were permitted to go on the coalface. Every week, I checked with the training officer to see when I could start my training.

Money was good compared to work outside of the Pit. My first wage was two pounds a week. Now that I was on three shifts and not earning as much money, I wasn't enjoying the job as much. The shift work interfered with my boxing and athletics' training. Shift work also affected my nights out with my mates too. I found it hard to go to work on the afternoon shift, especially after being at the beach in the mornings.

When I was in the Athletic Club, I was training three times a week, mostly in the evenings. I was told to keep up my running as I was setting up some good times. After spending a shift down the Pit, it did not seem worth bothering. Work had to come first. This was my third job to speak of and I was only 17-years-old. With a little encouragement from my parents, I might have kept training. I really missed running. I clocked 52 seconds doing the 400 yards. The world record at the time was 47 seconds. I thought I might get back into it later.

One of the older lads from the Pit organised trips to Ramsgate on Saturday nights to the Coronation Ballroom. Most Saturdays, they had big bands on. That is when I started to drink with my other mates. I didn't keep up my dancing lessons, as I wasn't much of a dancer. I liked just drinking with my workmates when we went to Ramsgate.

One Saturday, my mate Ray and I decided to ride over to Margate. We did not have good bikes. There was always something missing on the bikes. Whilst Ray had a front light on his bike, I didn't. By law, you had to have a front light.

After a long day and on the way back from Margate, Ray got a bit carried away, getting some way in front of me. As it was dark, I could not see where I was going. I failed to see a bend in the road and finished up hitting a brick wall. It did not do the bike any good. I ended up having to walk home. It was daylight by the time I got back to Deal.

A craze during this time was to wear American country and western shirts. On Saturday nights when we went to Folkestone to the skating rink, we would call into a little café in the Old High Street and have beans on toast. This cost one shilling and sixpence. We travelled to Folkestone by train, usually on a Saturday afternoon. We would both be ready for a cup of tea when we arrived, wearing our cowboy shirts and looking flashy. Skating was good fun.

The skating rink was on the seafront in Folkestone. The last train back to Deal was at 10pm. We could not miss that one, as Folkestone was 17 miles from Deal. We didn't go every week, as most weeks we would go dancing to either Ramsgate or Dover.

Most of my mates had push bikes. Some of them had good ones. There were no cars in those days, at least for young 17-year-olds. Not many men at the Pit had cars, either. Even my father never got a car. They all used Pit buses to take them to work.

I felt the pubs must have been better in Dover than in Deal. Dover was a garrison town. There were always three regiments stationed in Dover, whereas Deal had the marines. Dover had problems with the three different regiments, because there was a lot of rivalry amongst the soldiers.

There would be a gang of us that would catch the 6.30pm train to Dover from Deal. Most would be lads from the Pit and a few girls from the Pit canteen. We would go for a drink before going to the Co-op Hall or the Town Hall. We usually went to the Co-op as we found the Town Hall a bit upmarket and was a shilling dearer. Anyway, the pubs were not as good near the Town Hall.

The Co-op Hall Dance would finish at 11.30pm. The last train back to Deal was 11pm. It was an eight-mile walk if you missed this train, which I often did. We would always call into the Castle café to have a ham sandwich and a cup of tea before walking up the Castle Hill, which was steep at that time of night. If we were lucky, we would get a lift. If not, it was a long walk home.

Most of my mates from the Pit would always meet at the Deal Ice Cream parlour on the seafront. Not to eat ice cream, but to drink cups of tea. Sometimes, a cup of tea would last over an hour. The owners of the Ice Cream parlour did not mind. It was just as well as we would use the Ice Cream parlour all year. During the summer months it would be full of holidaymakers, mostly old people that would come to Deal for their holiday.

Living in Deal was good. The house was great. We lived close to the town centre and only a couple of hundred yards to the beach and Deal Castle. It was handy being within walking distance to the shops. Deal had a lovely promenade extending some two miles to Walmer Castle. This was a big castle, and like Deal Castle, overlooked the beach. I have many good memories of Deal. My Uncle was the first ever Labour councillor as Deal was a very conservative place.

My mother and father always went out on a Saturday night. They either went to the West Street Working Men's Club or went old-time dancing. In later years, my mother joined the Women's Dart Team. My father liked to go to the club on a Sunday morning to play dominoes.

The club would close at 2pm. I can still see my father walking home after closing time with a bottle of stout in his pocket for my mother—a sort of peace offering, as my mother would have had her dinner by that time. She always left the washing up for him to do.

I even joined the Betteshanger Male Voice Choir. My mate, Ray, belonged to it as well. I gave it a go, but I could not see myself singing in front of anyone. As such, it only lasted a few months for me. If we had gone to a bar for a drink before each rehearsal, I am sure we would all have sung better. Betteshanger also had a good brass band, but that never appealed to me to try it out.

Deal Boxing Fair (1951)

I was still training at the Boxing Club. Initially, I didn't do a lot of boxing fights, but I did box at the Deal Fair. The Fair would come to town in summer for the Deal Regatta. They set the Fair up in the park on the seafront and we boxed in a large tent with an authentic boxing ring. It had a big stage at the front of the tent where all the boxers at the Fair stood to take any challengers. You only had to stay the distance, being three rounds with them. The Fair boxers were usually ex-professionals and were paid by the Fair.

I remember once when I walked up the steps to make a challenge with a particular boxer, and the promoter would not let me box him. He said I was too big, which surprised me, as I was only about 10 stone. Instead, he offered me to box Mo Read. Mo was bigger than me and a few years older. What could I do but accept the challenge?

The crowd and my mates were cheering me on. If I managed to stay the distance, we would have some money—only a pound, plus whatever the crowd had thrown into the ring. We then could go for a pint to the pub across the road. I stayed the distance, receiving my pound and the change from the crowd. Later, I found out that Mo Read was boxing the following week at one of the big halls in London.

I had to end my boxing and gave up the Athletic club when I moved onto three shifts. I found this hard, especially the night shift. In the summer months, most of the lads I worked with cycled to the beach in the morning before going to afternoon shifts. Swimming at the beach was fun.

I had just turned 18-years-old when my mother had another baby boy, David, on the 28th of February 1952. *Dad was very proud of his youngest brother and loved him very much.* My mother was 37-years-old and my father was 43-years-old. At least I didn't have to run to the Pit to meet my father coming home from work this time. I certainly could have done so if it was required being a very fit lad.

The birth of David was quite a big surprise to us all, especially my sister Sonia, as she was no longer the baby of our family. I was still inclined to spoil Sonia, being only six-years-of-age. If she cried too much, I took her to the Ice Cream parlour to buy her a Knickerbocker Glory. It cost me two shillings and sixpence. I remember her holding my hand all the way to the Ice Cream parlour and back.

So now I had two brothers and a sister. Luckily, we had a big house. Had we still been living in Walton; it would have been a little crowded. Douglas was still at school and Sonia had just started school. I was now working three shifts at the Pit.

It was difficult for me when I was on night shift and day shift. On day shift I would have to be up at 5am and, being only 18, it was difficult to creep around the house, trying not to wake anyone up. I did not have a lot to do with my baby brother, David. I was at the age of having plenty to do. From the time I left home to work and come back was at least 10 hours.

Upon reflection 49 years later, since first moving to Deal, I find it has hardly changed. It's still a lovely, clean and picturesque seaside town. Although the pebble beach is hard to walk or sit on now, as teenagers, it didn't bother us at all. Of all the places I have ever lived in the world, Deal would be my favourite. I loved what Deal offered me in my youthful years as I grew up there and had so much fun. I could walk down the street and would always meet someone that I knew.

Smartly dressed in London.

4
MILITARY NATIONAL SERVICE

Recruit School (1950)

At 18 years of age, most of my schoolmates had been called up for compulsory National Service: the Army, Navy or Airforce. If you were learning a trade; electrician, carpenter, plumber, or mechanic, you would have to continue your trade after your two years of National Service. The only people exempt were those working in coal mines or on farms. *Enforced military conscription in England was abolished in 1960.*

My friend, Jimmy, left the butcher shop and joined the Grenadier Guards, the regiment that I once said that I would join one day. Signing on for three years meant you were paid more money than if you only signed on for two years. Jimmy was a few months older than I and he didn't like working in his father's butcher shop, so signing on for three years seemed like a good idea. His dad would not let him work down the Pit. Joining the Armed Forces was one way to see the world, which sounded appealing to young lads.

I began to think about joining the Army and when I spoke to my parents; I did not get any opposition because they knew I could not settle at the Pit. At the time, there were a lot of the lads joining the Army and they knew my mate Jimmy had already joined the Grenadier Guards. I put my notice in at the Pit. I had a lot of people trying to stop me from leaving the Pit. First, the Manager tried, then the Union and a few my good mates. My mate, Ray, had met his future wife at a Butlin's Holiday Camp and wanted me to be his best man at his wedding before I left for the Army. Yes, I got to his wedding, being very proud to be his best man.

I travelled to the Recruiting Office at Canterbury hoping to join the Grenadier Guards. As a boy, it was the regiment I said I would join but never really thought it could come true, but here I was, signing up. Once signed up, I immediately received a "Queen's Shilling". A pound would have been much better, as a shilling could only buy me one pint.

At the time of joining the Brigade of Guards, I didn't realise what discipline might entail. Of all the regiments in the British Army, it was the Grenadiers who were known to be disciplined the hardest.

I was not joining for the money, because in those days the money in the Army was not good. The food was not much to speak of either, but now I had signed up, there was no changing my mind. They gave me a week to prepare myself to make the journey to Caterham Barracks, not far from London.

From Deal, I had to catch two trains to get there. It was not worth packing much as I was going to be in uniform soon. I set off to Caterham with my small case, just shaving gear and a few odds and ends. I was in for a bit of a shock.

In June, I arrived at the Caterham Barracks Recruit School being met by the Sergeant of the Guard. I stood there shaking in my shoes. He asked me what regiment I was joining. Lucky for me, he was a Grenadier Guard Sergeant. He took the piece of paper with my particulars on them and told me to follow "that soldier". I thought all I needed to do was to keep up with him by just walking beside him. Well, it was not that easy. I had to run to keep up with him. I'm sure I wondered what had I let myself in for. Being only 18 and four months, I felt consoled knowing my mate Jimmy was somewhere in those barracks. They put me in a room with some Irish men that were joining the Irish Guards. One of the first things you are told upon arrival is your Army number. You are only told once.

I don't know if it was for our benefit, to let us know what to expect, but from our barrack room window, we could see the recruits being marched up and down. We all went to bed that night wondering what had we all let ourselves in for. The next morning, when we woke up, which was very early, we found that the future Irish Guardsmen had second thoughts. I expect they were on the next ferry back to Ireland. They must have had a change of heart.

While at Recruit School, a few of the recruits went absent without leave having no intention of coming back. The Military Police would find the recruits and swiftly return them back to the Army. That was one thing about the Army, you could not put your notice in, to leave Recruit School.

Sunday nights we would touch our gear up, getting it ready for Monday morning marching drills on the parade ground. When cleaning our gear in the barracks, we would have to sit with our legs across the bed, not speaking, unless the trained soldier spoke to us first. As lights were out at 10pm, it meant we had to retreat to the toilets to finish cleaning our gear. Sometimes I stayed there until after midnight. Our boots were the hardest things to clean, as you had to see your face shining back at you like a polished mirror. We used an old toothbrush and a candle to get all the rough parts off our boots. Then we used Blanco, a cleaning and colouring product, on our belts. Our uniforms were pressed every day.

Most of my Army wage went into buying cleaning materials for my gear, which we bought at the canteen. If we were lucky, we could buy ourselves a cup of tea and maybe a cake. It was a nice place to sit as you were away from the barrack room. There were about 25 men in each barrack room, which was usually the complete squad.

We had to be back on parade ground again in the afternoon if we didn't get it right in the morning. So that meant cleaning our gear twice on some days. Our Drill Sergeant was not overjoyed about having us on the square again, as he had a reputation to keep. Our boots were very important, but once they were at a good standard, they were easier to keep clean.

My Drill Sergeant was a man called Sergeant Day. Should we do anything wrong on the parade ground, he would shout at us and call us "horrible men". Mind you, we did some wrong things in our first few weeks, but as time went on, it was not too bad. I felt sorry for the new recruits that came after us. Towards the end of the 12 weeks, we certainly got better.

One of the things they made us do on the parade ground was to stand facing the wall at six inches off then on the order, we would have to "slope our rifles". You had to get it right first time otherwise you would have some very sore knuckles from scraping the brick wall.

The Officers did not have it all their own way. They had to always be smartly dressed. Their training was at Sandhurst. At this time, the Officers had to buy a commission to be an Officer in the Guards. They always came from "well-to-do" families, mostly gentry of the land where their fathers had also been officers in the Guards. The Regimental Sergeant Major gave them a hard time. The officers then gave the Sergeants a hard time, so we, the recruits, would end up at the end of the big stick.

Now in the Army, I could start boxing training again. The Drill Sergeant asked if any of us boxed in "civvy street". I told him that I had. As sport was very important to them, I was allowed to train every afternoon in the gymnasium.

The Grenadier Guards had chosen a boxing team to fight the Irish Guards. I was to fight a man called Harris, who had been the London champion. The Drill Sergeant told me that if I won, he would arrange for me to have a 36-hour pass. I won that fight and so the next day I received my pass. I felt really pleased with myself as they stopped the bout in the third round. That was the only fight I had at Caterham Recruit School.

At Caterham, I was able to restart my athletic training. They had a good track there to train on. While I was there, the Grenadier Guards won a championship cup. I was chosen to receive the cup from Prince Henry the Duke of Gloucester (1928-1974 House of Windsor).

My first weekend at home was good. My parents noticed I had changed. I suppose the haircut was a bit of a give-away. I went to the club with my dad dressed in my uniform. My father treated me to a couple of pints. We were given a railway warrant (free pass for train travel) for our first 48-hour leave. That being about all I had; my father slipped me a pound to go back with. We returned to the barracks late on Sunday afternoon. I travelled with Jimmy, as he was in the same squad as me.

One of the dreaded things was to have a kit inspection carried out by the Officer of your squad. We had to stand by our bed, shout out our name and our Army number, then allow the Officer to inspect our locker and check our clothes. They even checked our shaving tackle. If they found anything wrong, they marched you in to see the Adjutant (military administration officer) the next day. This meant we could find ourselves working in the cookhouse after the drill parades, or they would call "extra fatigues" on the square in the afternoon. We would be chased all over the square for a whole hour. Usually that would be on a Saturday afternoon, which was not fun when your mates were going out. I must admit, I have done a few extra duties on the parade ground. The term was called "foot bashing" and it was well and truly foot bashing.

We all felt very relieved after the 12-week pass out of Caterham Barracks, as the next part of the training was at Pirbright in the County of Surrey. The six weeks of training were mostly field training. We were taught all about guns; being shown how to fire them, including taking the guns to pieces and rebuilding them. We still had foot drills, but not as much. There were all kinds of assault courses to complete in certain timings. We would run miles with all our gear in big backpacks. I really enjoyed that part of the training.

I liked this type of training so much that the Major asked if I would join the Guards Parachute Regiment. One of my mates had joined the Parachute Regiment and I think he probably put a word in for me. Having seen what they do for training, I thought I would give that one a miss. I often saw about 12 of them running along the road carrying a big tree trunk. I may have got away from the square bashing, but jumping from an airplane is not something I could have ever seen myself do. At least they gave me a choice, which was very rare in the Guards.

My six weeks at Pirbright were incredibly enjoyable. One of the funniest things that I came across at Pirbright was when I was doing guard duty at the camp with another soldier. He recognised my Yorkshire accent and asked where I was born. When I told him "Walton, Yorkshire," he said he lived across the road from me. His older sister took my sister out for walks. He was in the Coldstream Guards. That was the regiment that most Yorkshiremen joined. Jimmy and I were the odd ones out. We were in the wrong regiment. Too late now, the Grenadier Guards had acquired two cheeky Yorkshire lads.

We seemed to get more time off there and were able to go out a bit. On pay day, Thursday, we would head down to Guildford for a drink. We could also get a pint in the Pirbright canteen. The canteen was only for the Guards. This made for a more relaxing time, as we could undo our ties a bit. Pirbright was not far from London, so sometimes we went there on the weekends if we weren't rostered on guard duty. We had to be careful getting back to camp after a night out. If we were late back, we would have to spend a night in the Guardroom and if it happened to be a Saturday night, then you were left there until Monday. You had to look as if you had not had too much to drink.

To receive our wages, we had to stand in line. When our name is called out, we would stand to attention, march forward, then salute the Officer to collect our wage. I don't suppose they have to do that now, as I think wages would go straight into their bank accounts. At Pirbright, I found that I had more of my wage left. I no longer needed to buy so much cleaning material. We were able to go to the canteen every night to have a cup of tea or if we felt well off; we could have a pint on payday.

Once we had finished our six weeks at Pirbright, they sent us up to Yorkshire to a small market town called Pickering. It was a lovely little town. There was a lot of snow around winter, particularly on the moors, and it was very cold. Our camp was next to the Castle, which consisted of a few huts that we had to sleep in. There was no form of heating in the huts. We spent most of the day on the moors. During one of the two weeks, we stayed on the moors and lived in the trenches surrounded by snow.

Not that we got much time to visit the pubs of the town but when we did, we found the Pickering pubs very friendly. It may have been because we were the only soldiers there. There would have been about 25 of us.

Having finished our two weeks in Pickering, we were now classed as trained Guardsmen. We headed back to Pirbright before being sent on to our battalion. At that time there were three battalions: the 1st at Wellington Barracks, the 2nd Battalion at Chelsea and the 3rd in Germany. Jim and I were hoping to be sent to the 2nd Battalion in London. Before they posted us to any of the battalions, we were given leave.

2nd Battalion (1953)

Jimmy and I were both posted to the 2nd Battalion in London at Chelsea Barracks in January 1953, which was a short walking distance from Trafalgar Square. Moving to London meant we had more gear to keep clean, as we were always in full view of the public. The uniform was different from what we had at Recruit School. It now consisted of a scarlet tunic with a lot of brass buttons on it, a bearskin that we had to keep regularly groomed (Canadian black bear fur caps), boots that you could see your face in, white belts and a rifle to keep polished.

They placed us in a barrack room that had soldiers who had been in the Army for a few years. They knew the ropes, so they were a lot of help to us new recruits. I made loads of friends. I found they had discovered all the tricks, including showing us quicker ways to clean our gear.

The barrack room was upstairs at Chelsea Barracks. When we had to come down to go onto the parade ground, we all walked stiff legged so that we would not crack our boots. We even walked stiff legged across the parade ground. If anyone had seen us and did not know why we did that, they would have thought we had not got to the toilet in time. We helped each other by brushing our scarlet tunics down. This part of the day was very important. If your turn-out was not good enough, it could mean being held in the guardroom. Alternatively, you may spend a few hours in the cookhouse or even being confined to barracks for a few days.

We were required to guard Buckingham Palace, The Tower of London, St James Palace and the Bank of England. If any Heads of State came to London, we would line-the-Mall if the Head of State had an audience with the Queen. London was going to be "a spit and polish" place for Jimmy and me.

One of the things that brought people to London was the pomp and ceremony. Tourists from all over the world came to see The Changing of the Guard at Buckingham Palace. The 2nd Battalion had a very busy year ahead in 1953. We were involved in the Queen's Coronation in June, the opening of the houses of Parliament in October and all the other times when we were required to line-the-Mall for visiting Heads of State.

Being inspected was critical. We had to make sure our bearskin was well groomed and the scarlet tunic was looking perfect with crystal clear brass buttons shining. You were allowed to have a moustache, but if it was just starting to grow, you had to pencil it in darker. At the inspections, I would have loved to have had my parents see me. They never saw me in my full scarlet uniform. The inspections took 30 minutes. We always folded our sheets and blankets neatly and placed them at the bottom of the beds all day. If my memory serves me correctly, we were not allowed to make our beds until about 4pm.

After the inspection, we marched behind the band and through the back gate of the barracks, being led by the Police on their horses all the way. We would march down Victoria Parade to Buckingham

Palace into the forecourt of the palace. This is where The Changing of the Guards (changing from the old guard to the new guard) is carried out, taking up to an hour, being watched by the crowds of tourists. I loved marching behind the Guards' Band when they were used for Changing of the Guard at Buckingham Palace. This was one of my most favourite duties.

In those days, the Guards stood out in front of Buckingham Palace. There were not as many tourists then as there are now. We would do two hours at the front and then have four hours off. The four hours' break would mean getting your gear ready for your next duty. During those four hours, we would get something to eat or try to have some sleep.

On some days during the summer months, it would be hard being on duty, as wearing the bearskin felt hot and heavy. The brass strap that went around the chin would be uncomfortable at times, too. We wore a white shirt under our scarlet uniform. I have known soldiers to faint in the heat. I was lucky that never happened to me.

I would love to have a pound for every time my photo was taken guarding the palace. Only the Policemen pocketed any money in the transaction. Tourists would usually ask a Policeman if they could take your photo. If I had pocketed a pound for each photo, I would have been a rich soldier. A photo of me is probably in quite a few holiday snap photo albums around the world now.

To do guard duty at Buckingham Palace was usually a 24-hour guard, if the Queen was in residence. If she was not in residence, then we would do a 48-hour guard. After a 48-hour guard, it was good to go out, as you knew that you wouldn't be doing another guard for a couple of days.

As it was winter, I wore my grey coat over my tunic. We always wore them in the winter. One night, a tourist pushed a bottle of beer into my coat pocket. It was well received, but luckily this kind gesture was not discovered.

Alison Simpson

The milkman would go past at about 3am with a horse and cart into the palace. We enjoyed sloping our rifles to salute the milkman, as it was quiet. We would have gotten into trouble if we were caught.

An inspecting Officer gave me a credit for my turn-out while on guard at one of the sentry boxes. However, it was soon taken away from me, as I had changed with my mate from the next sentry box.

Tourists always wondered how we knew when to march up and down. It was quite simple. We would bang our rifle on the ground, and because it had a brass cap at the bottom, the sound travelled along the pavement. We would both count to 10, then take one-step forward, turn to face each other, then march towards each other. While marching towards each other, we would signal with our fingers when we were going to stop. I managed to get that to a fine art.

Marching towards each other had its problems outside Buckingham Palace, though. Tourists would sometimes get in the way. If they did, the Policemen had to move them out of the way. Once you had made the signal to the Guardsman that you were going to march up and down, you couldn't change your mind. There were no mobile phones or discreet earpieces in those days. Other guard duty locations I had no trouble with, it was only at Buckingham Palace as the crowds were very big. We were advised to stay in our sentry boxes as much as possible to avoid any mishaps.

Years later, I found out that the Officers of the battalion had recorded me as a non-commissioned officer material. They obviously thought I was intelligent and capable for the role of Officer. My weekly wage was two pounds, 12 shilling and ninepence. Overtime was never available, so I could never increase this amount.

One time when the Queen came over to inspect us at the back of Buckingham Palace, she stopped to speak to the Guardsman standing right next to me. I must say, I was most pleased she was talking to him and not to me. I was too nervous. I'm sure my grandchildren would not be so nervous as I was then. I love that I can say I have slept at Buckingham Palace overnight. However, it was only in the guards' room, but still not many people can say that, I'm sure.

The Bank of England guard duty was an unusual one. There were long hallways to keep guard. We would get paid an extra shilling for that guard, which we had to sign for. It was enough to buy a pint of beer. If we had a pint of cider, it would only cost nine pence a pint. When our money ran out and we could not buy a pint of beer, we would settle for a pint of cider. This was not uncommon a few days after payday.

Guarding the bank started in the 18th century because an impending attack on the bank was expected. This guard duty ended in 1972, probably because of the amount of car traffic compared to when it first started. When I did the guard, we didn't stop for the traffic or red traffic lights and luckily no one was knocked down.

The best guard duty was at the Tower of London because you didn't get the crowds there. At most sentry boxes, you were there by yourself. This made it much easier to march up and down, whenever you felt like it, without having to signal the next Guardsman. We marched there from Chelsea Barracks, having to be at the Tower of London at 11.30am. There was one Officer to 22 men. The main function at the Tower was the Key Ceremony. It was a public duty that has been performed for the last 700 years.

I had the opportunity to "Challenge the Keys". The Chief Yeoman, Beefeater, carried the keys. You heard him coming as he rattled the keys. The Yeoman would come along with four other members of the Guard. One would be carrying a lantern and the Chief Yeoman would be making a noise with his keys. It is done the same way every night at 10pm.

As a Guard, I would ask, "Halt, who comes there?"

"The keys," the Beefeater responded.

"Whose keys?"

Alison Simpson

"Queen Elizabeth's keys."

After which I would finish by saying, "Pass Queen Elizabeth's keys—all is well."

Then the trumpeter would sound the last post. The Yeoman, wearing a Tudor bonnet, took it off and waved it above his head. All this would be done with me challenging my rifle.

At the Tower, they kept six raven birds. This has been a tradition since the Tower was built. They live for about 25 years. The ravens do not leave because they have their wings clipped, preventing flight. When one dies, they are replaced from Scotland.

The Tower of London is where Anne Boleyn (second wife to King Henry VIII) was beheaded by her husband for treason. This marriage produced a daughter (Queen Elizabeth I), but not a son of which Henry wanted. He then married Jane Seymour, who did produce a son for him.

It is said that Anne's ghost still haunts the Tower. It is believed she comes out at night near a wall where we had to do guard duty. It wasn't much fun standing near that wall at 2am. Would a big fit man be frightened? Definitely yes.

There was a time when I was doing guard duty at the Tower when Ava Gardner, who was a well-known beautiful American actress and singer, visited us. She came into the guardroom to meet the Guards while I was lying on the top bunk during my rest break. Ava Gardener (1922 - 1990) had three husbands: Frank Sinatra, Artie Shaw and Mickey Rooney.

I recall a funny incident when I was standing on duty at the front gate of the Tower of London. The Corporal gave me orders, one of which was that I must salute Queen Mary if she came to the Tower of London. At the time, we were surrounded by American tourists. The only thing was that she had died the week before on the 26th of May 1953. I had a difficult job to keep a straight face. I will never forget the expression on the faces of the American tourists. Queen

Mary was the grandmother of Queen Elizabeth II, who was awaiting her coronation in June 1953.

We needed a pass from our Colonel to go out when not on guard duty. Getting the pass was a well-manoeuvred plan. In London, the Guards always had to look smartly dressed not just in uniform but in civilian clothes as well. To go out in civilian clothes, we needed permission. We marched to the Colonel of the battalion with the civilian clothes we hoped to wear. If he thought we were not presentable, we would not have permission to leave the barracks.

I remember one Guardsman who would walk out in his civilian clothes wearing a pinstripe suit with a Bowler hat. The Officers were not too pleased that he also had a walking stick, but what could they do, as he was quite presentable. Unlike me, he had no trouble getting past the Sergeant of the Guard.

Another Guardsman called "Lowery" who came from Liverpool, walked across the parade ground holding a dog lead, pretending that he had a dog on it. If we were on the parade ground getting ready to be inspected for guard duty, we would find it hard to keep a straight face. The Drill Sergeant would really blow his top. In the end, they made him see the Army doctor. When the doctor told him to take a seat, he would put the end of the dog's lead on the seat and just stand there. In the end, they discharged him on medical grounds. I believe he had his full senses, as I know he could speak several languages. In those days, you could buy yourself out of the Army if you had the money. National Service was not everyone's cup of tea.

There were times when we watched for our Sergeant to go into the guardroom before making a dash for the front gate. We managed to get that off to a fine art. Being stationed in London had many good points. I saw lots of big shows that were held in London.

While I was stationed in London, one of my mates planned to get married. He asked me to be his best man. We were given permission to wear our scarlet uniform and our Bearskins to the wedding, which was being held in Oxford. I thoroughly enjoyed that weekend.

My wardrobe was limited, so I didn't mind wearing my uniform out of the barracks. Being in uniform had its advantages. When the opportunity came for me to get home for a weekend, I would have to hitchhike. The uniform helped. I did it a few times. I walked over the bridge next to Westminster Abbey onto Old Kent Road, kept walking as far as I could before I would put my hand up for a lift. Drivers were always happy to help someone in uniform. My father would pay for my fare back to London.

On leave, I would go to the West Street Working Men's Club with my mother and father. My father would give me money to go out on a Saturday night. I am sure they were proud of me. I only wish they had seen me in my scarlet uniform, but that would have been difficult in those days with Dad working at the Pit all week.

Deployment (Canvey Island and Isle of Sheppey)

The start of 1953 was a busy time for our battalion. Many of us were sent to assist workers after the deluge of flooding from the North Sea storm on the 31st of January. *The sea level rose to a further 5.6 metres, washing over the low-lying lands all along the east coast of England. The rising sea level affected other countries, including Belgium, Netherlands and Germany.*

On Canvey Island, sadly, 59 people lost their lives and 1300 were evacuated from their homes. It was our job to fill sandbags. Sometimes we were standing in the ocean to beat the incoming tides. It was heavy work and February (winter) was very cold. Nevertheless, it was a change to get away from public duties. If we were clean-shaven, we were left alone. During our stay there, we were billeted at a school. That became our home for over a week.

Army Squadron [Grenadier Guard] dress uniform.

Scarlet [Grenadier Guard] formal uniform.

Alison Simpson

Sgt T Day's Squadron at Guards' Depot, August 1952.

Boxing at welter-weight, weighing in at 10 stone.

5
SPREADING WINGS

Falling in Love

When we finished at Canvey Islands, we were given a weekend off. This was well received, as we only got a few weekends off each year. On the Saturday of that weekend, being 14th February, St Valentine's Day, together with a few old mates from the Pit, we went to Dover for some fun.

The first port of call was the pub called "The Grapes". It was a few doors away from the Co-op Hall, where the Saturday night dances were always held. We called at the pub first to give us a bit of "Dutch-courage" when it came to ask girls for a dance. We could buy soft drinks at the dance, but we were not soft drink lads. The lads of my age that still worked down the Pit looked forward all week to the Saturday night drink.

Girls that went to the dances at the Co-op must have found it a bit boring until we arrived just before 9.30pm. If anyone went out of the dance hall after 9.30pm, they were not allowed back in again. If we didn't feel like staying, we would head back to the pubs. The Red Lion was another pub that was also very popular with us.

This night being St Valentines, I felt like asking one of the girls to dance. She was wearing a green flowered skirt and standing with a group of other girls. Her name was Joan Sylvia Pearson.

One of the most popular songs of that day was *How much is that doggy in the window*. Well, I don't know if it was my singing or my dancing; I wasn't very good at either, but she let me walk her home. It meant a long walk for me as it was in the opposite direction to my walk back to Deal.

The dance finished at 11.30pm, and the last train to Deal was 11pm. Deal is nine miles from Dover. Joan lived two miles from Dover, in the opposite direction, so I had an 11 mile walk home at midnight.

We talked about where we were during the war. When I found out that we had both lived in the same small village up in Yorkshire, Moorends, we were both astounded. As I left Joan at her door, I invited her to Deal the following day to meet my parents. That was the first and only girl that I ever invited home to meet my parents.

The next day, my new girlfriend, Joan, met my parents. She was very nervous. That girl is now Grandma to our six grandchildren, *and ten great-grandchildren with more yet to come*. From then on, I tried to get home every weekend from London. That was not always possible. Most times, I had to hitchhike. I don't think that the Queen would be impressed if all her Guardsmen went home every weekend to see their girlfriends. We still had to do guard duties in London, even on weekends.

Boxing for the Battalion

In the winter of 1953, I was chosen to box for the battalion, which negated most of my guard duties. I spent a lot of time in the morning training in the gym. Some mornings, we would run along the embankment of the River Thames. Often, we called in to the café for a cup of tea, then run through the back gate of the barracks, pretending that we had run for miles. The person who trained me also chose the Army Boxing Team. He arranged many fights for me in London.

I was boxing more regularly in London then and was enjoying it very much. There were plenty of boxing clubs in London. Most of the English Champions boxed here. I made my way to the boxing halls on my own, unless another member of the battalion was boxing, too. Sometimes I needed to use seconds (the corner attendants, usually a trainer or an assistant) from the club I was boxing at, as I did not have my own assistant.

One evening, I boxed the Metropolitan Police Champion, knocking him out in the third round. As I came out of the ring, I was greeted by some of the front row spectators who suggested I should box at the Harringay Arena, North London, where all the big fights were held. For that fight, I won a lovely coffee set. On the bill that night was Henry Cooper's brother Jim. Henry Cooper was a British Heavy Weight champion and later knighted by the Queen.

Thursday night, payday, together with a few mates from the Guards, we would often visit the East End of London. We enjoyed a few drinks and a good singsong with the colourful locals. Sometimes the Pearly King and Queen would be there too, in their pearly outfits. It was quite a sight to see. *The "Pearlies" were elected leaders to collect money for charity in South London. They were responsible for keeping the peace and looking after their local communities, keeping them safe and well. The outfits were black suits, highly decorated with pearl buttons sewn onto them in patterns.*

In London during the 1950s, the Teddy Boy subculture became popular with young men after World War II. The style was influenced by the American rock-n-roll music scene inspired from country, rhythm and blues. The fashion had the Teddy Boys wearing long coats (drape jackets), high-waisted, narrow leg (drainpipe) trousers exposing the socks and pointed toe (winkle picker) shoes. Hairstyles were worn long using hairspray or grease gel to keep in place, with long sideburns.

We were never allowed to walk out of the barracks wearing Teddy Boy clothes. The downside was that some of the Teddy Boys did form gangs. We never had any trouble from them, though.

There was a dance called *The Creep*. It was banned in the Town Hall dances, but the Co-op Hall would play it. It was a dance that you could dance very slowly, shuffling along. In other words, you crept around closely with your partner. The Co-op Hall would dim the lights for this dance, which lasted for less than three minutes.

Now that I had a girlfriend, I tried to get home most weekends. Previously I had been hitchhiking to Deal from London but got fed up with this, as I never knew what time I would get home. Therefore, I started catching the train home. The problem with this, though, it left me short of money. As such, Joan and I would do a lot of walking when we got together.

One weekend, to save money, I rode to Dover with my mate Ray on our pushbikes. Before we left Deal, I told Ray where I was to meet Joan, this being at the bottom of Dover Castle Hill. When we got to the bottom of the hill, we were to turn right at the traffic lights. Looking smart in my uniform, we set off to Dover. Going down Castle Hill, I was the nearest to the pavement with Ray riding next to me. As I turned right at the bottom, he turned left, and we ended up in a big pile in the middle of the intersection. So much for looking smart and meeting my girlfriend. It would have been better to get the bus over to Dover at a cost of only one shilling and sixpence.

My bike was not a new one. It was mostly spare parts when I purchased it. Some of my mates had racing bikes. My bike was a pushbike but there were many times when I would end up pushing it, either because it had a flat tyre or because the Police were about. I often used my feet as brakes to slow down and the front and back lights rarely worked at the same time.

I resumed athletics training for the battalion, as I thought this would enable me to get out of more public duties. However, the battalion did not take athletics seriously, as they needed the men that summer. I recall an occasion where I entered a half-mile race, which I won easily. My Officer leaped with joy, throwing his hat into the air with excitement. I was lucky, as I had started athletics as a schoolboy and had accrued some experience. Unfortunately, the only other athletics

I did was during the Guards Recruitment School earlier in Caterham. *Nearly three decades later, I was a young 16-year-old wanting to get fit, so Dad, at 46 years old, took me for a beach run. He jogged effortlessly, while correcting my running style, and yes, he outran me with ease. I had a fit father that could outrun his teenage daughter. I was impressed.*

As I could not get home every weekend, my new girlfriend, Joan, decided to stop seeing me. Considering this, I just did not have the money to travel down every weekend I got leave, so I started spending most weekends in London. I know my father would have given me a pound if I needed it, but I felt that wasn't fair to my parents because I had made the decision to go into the Army.

Joan now had a Welsh soldier boyfriend. He was stationed in Dover. One Saturday, when walking around Battersea Park, I bumped into her again. She was with some of her friends from Dover. They were visiting London to see a show. We talked for a few minutes, but her friends kept walking on, so she had to rush to find them. Later that evening I met her again as she came out of the show *The Reluctant Heroes* at the Whitehall Theatre. The problem was, by this time, I had another girl on my arm.

After World War II, the region of Japan, Korea, China and Russia became involved in disputes over territory and political regimes. Korea fell victim to the Cold War and America was in control of Southern Korea, where the British soldiers were allies.

The Officers volunteered for us, that we could all go to Korea. We would have much preferred for all the Officers to go to Korea. Thankfully, by July 1953 a Korean Armistice Agreement was signed, being a peace treaty with China and North Korea until they could agree on a final peace settlement.

We now had to concentrate on getting ready for the Queen's Coronation. It was going to be a very big day. There was plenty of excitement leading up to the day. We had enormous amounts of rehearsals. We would be on the parade ground for many days. The

Trooping of the Colour and the Queen's Birthday were also on our calendar that required plenty of practice. During this time, we didn't get much time off. Our punishment would be spending time in the cookhouse if our performance was not up to scratch. The cookhouse was the last place I wanted to be after the coronation.

The 2nd of June 1953 was the coronation of Queen Elizabeth II. We were up very early to make sure our gear was spotless. We could see our faces in our highly polished boots, the buttons on our tunics shone brightly and our Bearskins were groomed to perfection.

We were on the parade ground early. From there we marched down to The Mall arriving about 8.30am, to line up along The Mall, which led directly to Buckingham Palace. I was posted opposite the Queen Victoria monument for most of the day.

The crowds had been there all night to get good positions. Unfortunately, it rained all day, so we had to wear our wet weather capes. No one could see all the good work we had done on our uniforms and our Bearskins just got wet.

I remember the Queen of Tonga had an open carriage. The rain did not bother her, so the crowds really gave her a big cheer. We were required to "present arms" (a form of salute) to all royalty that passed us. It was such a big occasion as many royal families came from around the world to witness the coronation of Queen Elizabeth II. We presented our arms many times.

People who stood behind me kept giving me sweets. I appreciated this. After a few hours, we were marched into St James Park to have our lunch and a break. After the parade was over, we had to march back to Chelsea Barracks. All we wanted to do then was to take our gear off and get out to enjoy the activities that were taking place in London. You couldn't move for tourists and the pubs were full.

After the Trooping of Colour at the Horse Guards Parade for the Queen's Birthday, there was one more major event to come, the State Opening of Parliament, in October.

One thing I always enjoyed was having a pot of tea when we got back to the barracks at night. If we had any money left, we would buy a meat pie from a pie van that parked behind the barracks at night. One place we frequently visited in the winter was a café just off Trafalgar Square, called Lyons Corner House. It was a big café. The food was cheap there, and it was open 24 hours a day. We called in there to get out of the cold. Sometimes they would turn us all out as they needed to give it a good clean out. It was not unusual to sit there for a couple of hours on some occasions. I suppose it was like a meeting place, like the Ice Cream parlour in Deal.

It was very rare for me to eat a meal out of the barracks. Occasionally, though, we would have a meal at the café if we could not get home for the weekend. I would not hang around the barracks if we were not expected to be doing any duties at the weekend. It was only about a 20-minute walk into London from the barracks.

The Nuffield Centre was for servicemen who, when in London, could call in for a bit of relaxation. One of the sayings about London was, "if you were tired of London, then you were tired of living". London was a great place to be in those days. I saw lots of shows. I never had to pay for the shows as I would usually get in for free by getting a ticket from the Nuffield Centre, near Trafalgar Square.

Deployment (Egypt)

It was about this time that we were told that the 2nd Battalion was going to Egypt to relieve the 3rd Battalion who were already there. This pleased me, as it did many others too. The year had been hectic, with many duties outside of Buckingham Palace. Being busy meant continuously cleaning our gear, something we did not enjoy. Going to Egypt would mean less gear to look after. Our uniform would likely be shorts and long socks. I didn't get home for Christmas in 1953, therefore I was looking forward to our embarkation leave, which was three weeks in February 1954.

My mate, Jimmy, was given what we would call a cushy job in the gymnasium at Chelsea. He then was given the same job at Caterham, back at the Guard's Depot. This meant he would not be going to Egypt with us. He only had 11 months left in the Army.

Going to Egypt in March 1954 left me with only 14 months to complete my three years of service. I would then be on the Reserve for four years, which meant I could be called up again should any conflict arise.

I had no idea what it would be like living in a tent for 14 months. Certainly not as good as living in the barracks. There was not as much gear to clean, and I now had some money left over out of my wages. I hoped that I could save some money for when I got out of the Army. I imagined that I would have a permanent suntan being in Egypt. As it turned out, we did not have time to get bored there.

While I was on embarkation leave in Deal, I went over to Dover to see if I could see my ex-girlfriend, Joan, coming out of her workplace. She worked in a big warehouse, Rowlands, as a packer. I caught her coming out of work with her friends. We talked for a while. I had been hoping that I could persuade her to write to me while I was in Egypt. Luckily, she agreed. From then on, Joan was pleased to be back with me again. We had a few days together before the end of the embarkation leave. I had recently turned 20 and Joan was 17-years-old. Joan often visited my parents whilst I was away in Egypt.

Canal Zone - Suez Canal, Egypt (1954-1955)

A treaty was signed in 1936 with the King of Egypt to maintain access through the Suez Canal for British trade and oil with the Middle Eastern countries but was repealed in 1951. The Egyptian people resented the British occupation of their land, and riots broke out in 1945. In 1953, Major General Muhammad took leadership of the country following a military coup. Later, Muhammad was ousted by Colonel Gamel Abdel Nasser in 1954. The British military withdrew from the cities to concentrate their presence next to the Suez Canal.

This area became known as the Canal Zone. By 1954, the garrison had grown to 70,000 troops.

Great Bitter Lakes - Guard Duty

It might seem that we did not do much while we were in Egypt, but in fact, we were very busy doing guard duty all over the place. One guard we did was near the Bitter Lakes. Our job was to search cars passing through. We stopped what could have been a taxi and made all the occupants get out. We counted 11 of them. Then we searched the taxi and came across a bottle of Black and White Scotch Whisky. We let them get back into the taxi, less the whisky. I don't know what happened to the whisky, but I suppose the Sergeant thought it had come from one of the Sergeant's mess tents.

Red Sea - Guard Duty

It was very hot living near the Red Sea. We had to be careful not to get stung by a scorpion. It was important to always bang our boots on the floor before we put them on, shaking out any scorpions that might have climbed in. While I was stationed in Egypt, the battalion arranged for us to have trips into Cairo to see the pyramids. As we had to pay for it ourselves, I never seemed to have enough money left over to get there.

Throughout my childhood, Dad often reminisced about Egypt and told me that I must visit this exotically beautiful place. It was in May 1992, aged 28, when I arrived in Egypt with my boyfriend, Gary and our two friends, Rob and Liz. The Egyptian leg of our trip was part of a three-month world tour the four of us had planned together. Upon arriving at Cairo airport on a late-night flight, our Egyptian Guide swiftly whisked us off to our hotel to check in.

With our hotel room keys in hand, we opened the door, walked past the two single beds and straight out onto the balcony, taking in the majestic view of the Nile River and city lights of Cairo. It was here, standing on the balcony, that I had achieved the mission of getting to Egypt for Dad. The thick humid air smelt very foreign to me. I burst into tears, crying at the joy of having arrived but also feeling an inner peacefulness of being home.

After Dad's missed opportunity to visit the pyramids, I made sure I got there for him. We went to the Giza Plateau, just outside of Cairo, in the Sahara Desert, to visit the famous pyramids and sphinx. At sunrise, our private group were able to climb inside the largest pyramid (Pyramid of Khufu) up into the King's Chamber to experience a sunrise meditation before it was open to the general public. This was an absolute highlight of my trip. Dad loved seeing all our photographs. He was so glad I had got there for him.

Tel El Kebir - Guard Duty

The Brigade Ordnance Depot was at Tel El Kebir. This place had a 28-mile barbed wire fence around it with watch towers, dogs and searchlights. Despite all these protective measures, local thieves still stole things. One night, George and I were patrolling the perimeter wire when we thought we would fire a few rounds, just to break the boredom. It was not long before the Sergeant with the Officer arrived in a jeep, wanting to know what happened. We both made the excuse that some of the local thieves had tried to get into the compound. We got away with that excuse because we were always told that we could fire to frighten people away but not fire to kill.

When working at the Brigade Ordnance Depot, we always took enough rations for a month. This would include beer. I recall one time when I had a few drinks with the cooks, the next day all the soldiers in the camp (about 50) except the four of us who had been drinking beer, went down with dysentery. All the sick men were ferried to the Army hospital, leaving behind the cooks and myself to look after the camp. That night, we noticed footprints from wild dogs in our tent. These wild dogs are called Pieard dogs, like dingoes in Australia.

I remember when a new batch of Guardsmen had just arrived from England. One person, who used to live in Dover, joined us for a drink.

He wanted to be one of the lads quickly, so he bought the first round. That was the last round he bought because he couldn't cope with the Egyptian beer. There were about six of us that night.

One night when the four of us went for a drink at Fayed on payday, we were amazed to see another 14 soldiers fighting over a RAF woman. It was quite a fight. There were very few women in Egypt when we were there.

Most Egyptians that worked in our camp were pleased that we were there, giving them a job. They did our washing and ironing for us. It only cost a few piastres (Egyptian currency). This sounds horrific now, but they filled their mouths with starch and water, spurt onto our Khaki drill uniform and iron. Whilst not very hygienic, they did a great job. We would have loved to have them work for us in London, where we had much more gear to clean and press.

As we were doing an exercise in the desert, some distance from our camp, our tent burnt down. Upon our arrival back at camp, we had to pay for all our Army gear that was lost in the fire. Luckily, my photos of Joan were in a steel box. I was not happy to pay for the Army gear as I had not been anywhere near the tent when it burnt down. Being in the Army, we had no choice. It cost me 30 pounds. That was a lot of money when you consider I was only earning three pounds a week. This unfortunately happened when I was trying to save for when I left the Army.

We did our fair share of drills, fatigues, and exercises in the desert. It was completely different from life in the big smoke of London. When on exercises in the desert, we often came across the Bedouins. This nomadic tribe would continuously travel around the deserts in North Africa, it was their way of life. We often gave them bread or any food we could.

When in the desert, we were only given a small amount of water with which we had to wash, shave and drink from. We found it very hard to manage this small amount that was issued to us, especially when we were down at the very hot area of the Red Sea. At the Red Sea, the most common meal was corned beef stew. By the end of the day, you would be ready to eat almost anything. I enjoyed the trips to the desert as it was good to get away from camp life.

When not doing exercises, I was given a job in the Guardsman's mess. I liked this job as it was near the cookhouse. This meant I could get some good meals. When the cooks were there, they gave me extra rations. This was good for me, as I kept up my boxing training. I would train at the side of the big cooking ovens, even though there was no boxing in the battalion at the time because of the tension in the canal zone.

When I worked in the mess, I often gave the Egyptian workers bread to take home. I gave them a note with it, because they could get into serious trouble if caught taking anything from the camp. My mate, George, was at the gate, so I knew they would get through ok.

One time, I went with some of the Irish Guardsmen to their camp in Ismailia. They had a good boxing team. I often wonder what would have happened to me if I had transferred to the Irish Guard regiment from the Grenadier Guard regiment. *The five regiments of foot guards are The Grenadier Guards, Colestream Guards, Scots Guards, Irish Guards and Welsh Guards.*

It was Colonel Nasser who had negotiated a withdrawal of the British Troops from the Canal Zone with a draft agreement drawn up and signed in October 1954. As a result, we had to be careful where we went. If we went out, we had to always go in pairs. The tension of British troops' presence in Egypt was high. We now needed to have eyes in the back of our heads.

Port Said

Our battalion moved to Port Said, a major port of Egypt on the Mediterranean coastline. It was a much better camp than the one at Fayed near the Great Bitter Lakes. Nevertheless, we still had to go out in pairs. A lot of places were out of bounds to us because of the continuing problems with some of the unfriendly population. There had been rioting for a few months, as some of the Egyptians wanted home rule introduced sooner than the specified date.

We often took the ferry across the Suez Canal from Port Said to Port Fuad. This place was designated for married families and was a holiday area. It made a pleasant change from the few shops in Port Said. It was in Port Fuad where I got a tattoo but I did not like it, so the tattooist didn't get paid.

Port Fuad was a good place to go for a drink as they served Scotch Beer there. Fortunately, we usually sobered up before we got back to our camp. One night, we must have disturbed some passengers on the ferry. When we arrived back at Port Said, the Military Police met us as we came off the ferry. They escorted us back to the camp to spend the night in the guardroom. The next day, the Commanding Officer gave the battalion a lecture about us, telling everyone to be good Guardsmen when out in Port Said. We were not allowed out for the rest of the week having to sit in the NAAFI (Navy, Army Air Force Institutes) each night. My drinking mates and I sat at one end and the rest of the battalion at the other end. No doubt we had been "sent to Coventry" (which means to be completely ignored by all others).

21st Birthday

While stationed at Port Said, I bought my girlfriend back home, Joan, some Egyptian drop earrings. She bought me a lovely wristwatch for my 21st birthday. That might have been the night that George, my best army mate in Egypt and I were escorted back to camp by the Military Police.

One night, George and I called into a café in Port Said for a drink. When George mentioned to the owner that I had done a bit of boxing for the battalion, the owner wanted to arrange a fight with one of the locals. Whilst a little tempting, there was no way I could have taken the risk. I doubt I would have come out alive, as the tensions between the Egyptians and the British had severely deteriorated.

They clearly wanted us to leave their country. I would have been in a considerable amount of trouble with the battalion if I had agreed to the fight. It was bad enough when George and I were escorted back to camp earlier by the Military Police. My feet would not have touched the ground if there had been a next time.

I was really surprised when I had finished my time in Egypt because the Commanding Officer asked me to sign on to stay there. By this time, I was keen to return to England and get back to Joan. She had been writing to me for the last 13 months. I was now an old-boy soldier and most of the mates I had were now leaving the Army too. Plenty of new soldiers had joined the battalion while we were in Port Said. Many of my mates had joined The Metropolitan Police in London.

I had never once given it a thought as to what I would do when I left the Army. I suppose I thought that there would always be the Pit again. As I intended to live in Deal, there weren't many job options to choose from.

I had completed about 13 months since the day we arrived in Port Said. It would take a few weeks by ship before disembarking at Southampton. Going home to be demobbed in England felt quite different. We were all looking forward to it and hoping for no Drill Sergeants this time. They did not bother us too much now.

On the trip home to Southampton, we were all planning to have a few pints of good quality English beer, as we had more than enough of Egyptian beer. On the ship we were quite disappointed as we thought the Navy was watering down our beer or the Egyptian beer was a much stronger brew. It was no good complaining because it was cheap beer and the Navy was running the bars.

My Army service in Egypt was enjoyable. I loved the times we spent in the desert. I would call it good soldiering. On the ship back home, I had plenty of time to reflect on my time as a soldier in London. I loved that too. We had to be smartly dressed at all times. Guard duties at Buckingham Palace were good, along with the other guards at The Tower of London and The Bank of England. Marching behind the Army bands was always uplifting for our spirits. I felt so proud of being a Grenadier Guard but now I was thinking of civvy street.

Before arriving at Southampton, we were told that Customs would come on the ship to check our belongings. There was a bit of a panic by some soldiers who had items that would not be allowed back into England. Going up the Solent Estuary towards Southampton, the sea was covered with the things that were discarded by the soldiers, not wanting to be caught. It was a waste of time, however, as the Customs people did not come on the ship.

In April 1955, we disembarked at Southampton and boarded a train for Pirbright. From there, we were to be sent home for a one-month leave before returning to Pirbright to be demobbed. I was really looking forward to this leave, as I was going to see Joan for the first time in 14 months.

I was given a Railway Warrant to Deal, but I caught the train from Charing Cross to Dover, where I was to meet Joan. We met outside The Poppy Inn, a restaurant just off the Market Square. This is where Joan often worked waitressing in the evenings with her mother.

It was late in the evening when I arrived at Dover. Unfortunately, I was not able to stay long as I had to catch the last bus back to Deal. Joan walked me to the bus, knowing that she too had to catch a bus home. I spent loads of time in Dover over the next four weeks. I would stand across the road from where Joan worked, waiting for her to come out.

Alison Simpson

Love from Arnold in Egypt, photograph sent to Joan, 1952.

Christmas in Port Said, Egypt.

Showing off his suntan, Egypt.

Drinking with the cooks, Egypt.

Arnold enjoying a drink out with his mate, Egypt.

Army mates on a night out in Fayed, Egypt.

6
CIVVY STREET

Deal Pier Labourer

While on leave, I managed to organise myself a job that started after leaving the Army. I would be working on the Deal Pier that they had just started to build. This entailed building in-between the sea tides. As it was summer, it was a good job to have as I loved being at the ocean. *Mum tells me that she often sat on the beach watching Dad work on the pier. Deal Pier III started construction in September 1954; three years later it was complete. HRH Prince Phillip, Duke of Edinburgh, officially opened it on the 19th of November 1957.*

In May 1955, I returned to Pirbright to get demobbed and collect my demob suit. It was not the best of suits as it was left over from the last war. I chose what I could and a hat, knowing full well that I wouldn't be wearing the suit or hat back in Deal. The hat was for Dad, as he loved wearing hats. When I got back to Deal, I had a new smart suit made for me, costing 22 pounds.

Alison Simpson

Courting Joan

I was regularly invited over to Joan's house for Sunday dinner (lunchtime). Usually, I cycled from Deal. Her mother always made plum pie every Sunday. I always accepted it, not having the nerve to say that I didn't like plum pie, because I wanted to be on my best behaviour all the time to impress. I was not keen with their version of Yorkshire pudding either, as they made it with self-raising flour, rather than plain flour, like my mother.

After dinner (lunch), Joan and I would go for bike rides before returning home for Sunday tea. I really enjoyed tea. It was usually ham and tomato sandwiches, followed by homemade cake. One of the funniest things regarding etiquette in their house was how I would help myself to the sugar for my tea, not knowing that it was Joan's mother's job to serve strict portions of sugar in her house. Joan and her sisters would hold back the giggling, trying to keep straight faces as I helped myself. They thought I was very brave to put my own sugar in my tea. My parents always let us put our own sugar in our cups of tea.

Joan's parents seemed quite strict in those days, compared to my parents, who were much more easier going. After my short spell away from home, with the Merchant Navy, then three years in the Army, I guess they would have found it a bit hard to tell a 21-year-old not to put too much sugar in his tea.

Our courting mainly consisted of going for walks along the cliffs or window-shopping. Window-shopping meant just looking in shop windows and dreaming together about what we would like to buy if we had the money. In those days, shops left their lights on in their front windows, as it was safe to do so. We would sometimes call into a nice pub for a drink. Joan would often have a port and lemon and I would have a pint of mild (beer). Often, we would have something to eat, a pork pie or Cornish pasty. In those days, pubs didn't sell counter lunches. On some Saturday nights, we would go to the West Street Workingmen's Club with my parents. On one occasion, Joan's parents came over to Deal to the club too. Sometimes, I would stay at Joan's house for the weekend.

While I was in Egypt, Joan had a bad accident at her workplace. One of the salesmen had left a big glass bottle of sweets on the floor, in the aisle walkway. She didn't see it and kicked it with her foot whilst she was carrying a box of groceries. Joan was taken to hospital by the warehouse owner, in his posh car. She had stitches for the injury and was given crutches. Joan was off work for a long time, unable to walk without the crutches. The funny thing was how her dog would lift one of his legs, hobbling on three legs when they went out for walks. It was a funny sight to see. There was a nasty scar from the stitches left on her foot. Not good for a young 17-year-old girl.

Back to the Pit

With the work on the Deal Pier finishing soon, I managed to get a job back at Betteshanger Pit. This time I had to make do with a job on the screens. It was not a very good job, and the money was poor. The job involved taking off any rock or stone that came along the steel conveyor. The conveyor belt ran non-stop and was very noisy.

Day shift would be from 6am until 2pm. It was a long time to stand in one place. At 10am the conveyor belt was stopped for a 20-minute break. We called it "snap time". I would usually have jam or cheese sandwiches, or if it was a Monday morning, it likely would be dripping (the oily juices from cooking meat that has been solidified into a spreadable texture) and salt sandwiches.

The job was hard in the winter, as it would get cold. I had to wear a cloth hat. Luckily for me, I was only on this job for a few months. There were a few like me who had just come out of the Army or Navy. Some who had married local girls and had been in the Marines in Deal too. It was such a poorly paid job that if you were married, you would have to go down to the National Assistance office (Social Security) to have your wages made up, to make a reasonable income. This was quite common for men that worked on the Pit top.

Most of these men would not go below ground because the men that worked underground had fathers that already worked there.

The only place to earn good money was at the coalface, as it was piecework. The harder you worked at the coalface, the more money that you would earn. It also helped if you had a good deputy. My father was a Deputy and the men that worked for him were the best-paid men in the Pit.

Wedding Day

Joan and I decided to get married on the 3rd of September 1955. Our wedding was at the Methodist Church in Snargate Street, Dover. It wasn't posh or a big wedding, just a few relatives and friends. My brother, Douglas, was my best man. Both Sonia and Joy were the bridesmaids, our sisters. I didn't have much money saved as I had to repay the Army for the lost gear out of my tent. The reception was held at Joan's home, not far from the church. *My parents coined the term "Mr H" and "Mrs H". They enjoyed using this expression throughout life when light heartedly referring to each other. Mum tells me Dad usually called her "sweetheart".*

After the reception my father-in-law said that he would take us all, including my mother and family, back to Deal in his car. This sounded good, as we rarely travelled in a car. However, Joan and I had to get out of the car halfway up Dover Castle Hill. The fully loaded car would not have made it up the hill otherwise.

This brought back old memories, as I had done this a few times when I had walked Joan home. I never thought I would be walking up Castle Hill with my wife on our wedding day. Lucky for us we had not been walking for long when someone stopped to give us both a lift back to Deal.

My brother John remembers Grandad Pearson (Mum's dad) had a blue Singer Gazelle. From 1956 to 1970, the Singer Gazelle was in production by the British Company, Singer. Our grandparents were the first family to afford a car in their estate, The Ropewalk. Grandad would often take his entire football team to their games, all piled in like sardines. He was an electrician's mate and Grandma worked as a waitress at this time. It was a rarity for married women to work in those days, but this would have helped them to afford a new car.

As the Pit closed for holidays in July each year, I could not take time off-work for a real honeymoon. We spent our honeymoon in Canterbury visiting my father, who was not able to attend our wedding because he was in hospital from a Pit accident. He almost lost his entire leg when it got stuck, from crawling over the conveyor belt, at the coalface.

We didn't have much money, but we managed to get a furnished two-room flat in the same street as my parents in Deal, costing two pounds a week. We were very lucky, as flats were hard to get. At least we didn't have to start our married life living with our parents. The flat had two rooms, a bedroom and a living-kitchen room. We had to share the toilet and bathroom.

It was a handy location, being near my parents. On one occasion, Joan ran along to my parent's house carrying a basin with flour and an egg, to ask my mother how to mix a Yorkshire pudding. From that day on, she has always made good Yorkshire puddings. We didn't stay there long because we did not like sharing the flat with mice, too. Soon we were looking for something better.

Growing up, Mum and her sisters were not allowed in the kitchen to learn how to cook. They could go into the kitchen only when it was time to clean up the dishes. So, Mum never knew how to cook meals when she got married. Mum remembers at school they only learnt how to make easy things like jam tarts.

My brother John had such a good memory. He reminded Mum and I of a lovely story where she, a newly married woman, was walking past a pork butcher shop and noticed the long queue of people waiting to be served. She thought it must have been a good butcher shop, so she joined the queue to buy a roast for Sunday. When she got to the counter, she asked for a leg of lamb (in a pork shop). The butcher smiled kindly and offered a small piece of a leg of pork. John was a butcher's apprentice in his earlier years, so he loved retelling this story.

The next flat we moved into was not far from the seafront of Deal. It was a furnished flat at the top of a house. The flat consisted of a lovely sitting room, a big bedroom, and a kitchen. We had to share the toilet and bathroom again, but no mice this time. This flat had a coal fire in the bedroom. We loved how it was only a short walking distance to the shops and beach. We were able to carry our shopping back to the flat easily. The owner of the flat always commented how clean Joan kept the stairs.

We did not stay there for too long, as Joan was now expecting our first child. We were worried, because most flats would not allow children in them and we didn't have enough room for a baby in the flat. Another reason why we didn't stay there was because there was nowhere to keep a pram. We were never told to get out, but Joan would have found it hard to get up the stairs carrying shopping and a baby.

We started looking for a house to live in. Having no furniture, we had to buy furniture on hire purchase. This was not easy on my wage. Hire purchase was not a thing my parents believed in. The saying was "if you did not have the money to buy it, you should save for it".

We managed to get our first house in Downs Road, Walmer. It was a nice house with a big garden. The rent was three pounds per week, which was a lot of money in those days. Fortunately, by that time, I was given a better job at the Pit. It was a 9am-5pm job, but I was able to work overtime on the weekends, earning three pounds for a Sunday morning shift. We bought a lovely dining room suit on hire purchase and were very proud of it.

Now that my lass was expecting our first child, we went to look for a pram. It was not going to be a second-hand one. We saw a lovely one in a shop in Deal. Typical of those days, it was a big pram. We decided to buy it knowing it was going to cost us both a lot of money, 27 pounds, at least two week's wages. The pram was grey with big wheels and I thought it was the best pram in Deal at the time. Pushing it along the pavement it would take most of the pavement up. One person commented that we should have a bell on it.

We had raspberries in the back garden, and my lass would turn the raspberries into lovely tarts. My mother had taught Joan how to make tea cakes too. One day Joan cooked teacakes and invited my parents over. Unfortunately, between them, they ate a lot before I got home from work. At least I could still smell them in the house.

I started a new job at the Pit. I had to crawl along the coalface with a long hosepipe. We would bore long holes into the coalface, put the hose pipe into the hole, then pump water in to reduce the dust for the colliers. It was another job nearer to my goal of being a coalface worker with better wages.

One time, when I was crawling along the conveyor belt, a pin in the belt went straight into my knee. It was stuck, so they had to stop the coalface working until they got me out of the Pit. I was taken to hospital to have the pin removed. There were a few red faces the next day when I went back to work. The Manager was more concerned with having to stop the work at the coalface than my wellbeing.

In those days, there was no such thing as a retirement age. We had some miners working well into their 70s. Many men kept on working until they died. The man that trained me was 75 when he was told to retire. Not long after he retired, he died. It was not the work that killed him, rather, it was being made redundant that did it.

The shift I now had at the Pit was a good one. It was what miners would call the "egg and ham" shift. The shift started at 9am, much later than the normal day shift. I think that is where the "egg and ham shift" name came in, for having time in the morning to cook a breakfast. There was no way anyone would want a cooked breakfast at 4.30am. During the shift, when it was time to eat your sandwiches, you would eat them wherever you were working. There was no such thing as soap to wash your hands, although sometimes you may find some water if you were lucky.

While living on Downs Road, Joan's parents would often come over when I was at work. In fact, we had quite a few visitors now that we were renting a house. I still cycled to work. It was more convenient for me, and it was better than waiting for buses.

Alison Simpson

It was good cycling home on a Sunday afternoon. I would pass the pubs closing at 2pm, seeing the men that I knew from the Pit. I often thought it would be nice to call into a pub and have a pint on my way home, but as it was nearly closing time, not much chance of that. Besides, I was ready for my roast beef and Yorkshire pudding. The wonderful aroma from the Sunday roasts cooking as I cycled past the houses was enough to get me home very quickly.

We didn't have a television. In those days, we sometimes went to the Pictures or for walks to relax. Money was tight even though I often worked six days a week. Fortunately, the owners of the house had left a room with furniture. We tried to manage with what we had bought.

Happy days in London.

Deal seafront with Joan.

Wedding reception at 12 Ropewalk, Dover.

7
EARNING A CRUST FOR THE FAMILY

Paul

My lass went into the hospital on Sunday night. She was quite nervous, and I was also a worried young dad. Paul was not born until Tuesday the 20th of March (1956) at Bucklands' Hospital in Dover. A very long and frightening labour for a young woman. Joan was kept in hospital for 10 days, typical in those days, and I didn't want to take any risks of bringing her home too early. I cycled over each night to visit Joan and my baby son, Paul. Sometimes I got a lift in a car with the husband of the woman in the next bed to Joan.

Joan and Paul were picked up at the hospital by Joan's parents. I felt a little put out, as I would have liked to bring them both home myself. The first time that I ever held Paul in my arms, his nappy leaked. A young inexperienced mum was still learning.

In the 1950s, English society still believed it was a woman's job to fully care for the babies and children. It was rare to have a husband who helped change nappies. A man's societal expectation was to earn an income to support his family. The women had home duty responsibilities in providing care to the children and doing all the chores around the house, such as cooking, cleaning and nurturing the children. Grocery shopping was also a woman's job and men never carried a grocery bag, even if their wife was pregnant, which seems harsh from our perspective today.

It was common practice to leave a baby in their baby carriage (pram), outside the shop while you popped into the store to buy goods. Most shops were quite small, so bringing a baby carriage into a shop was not practical. Mum left Paul outside a shop in Dover and walked out through a different doorway. A few steps down the street, she realised she had left Paul behind. She spun around, rushing back to the shop, elbowing people out of the way, striding towards the other doorway where she had left Paul in his carriage.

We were a young family with several people commenting on our ages. Now I had a son. I wanted to get on the coalface to earn what they called big money. I would often call into the Pit office to see if they could rush it up. It would mean 120 days of training and during this time being unable to earn extra, having no chance of overtime. We were both managing ok, and the future looked good with the money I could earn on the coalface.

Joan went to the clinic every week to get Paul weighed and receive some advice. She was given orange juice for Paul's vitamin C levels that helped his immune system. My young brother David often visited us at our house on Downs Road. We sometimes brought him back with us, from my parent's house. David was only six-months-old when I joined the Army, so I never really had much to do with him. My lass had more to do with David than I ever did up until then. When he visited us, we tried to encourage him to drink the orange juice. Then we would stand him against the wall and pretend he had grown taller because of the orange juice.

Army Reserve Duty (Malta, Cyprus)

On the 26th of July 1956 Egyptian President, Nasser, announced the nationalisation of the Suez Canal Company, originally owned by the French and British interests. This was to help Egypt fund the Aswan Dam project by collecting the tolls from ships passing through the Suez Canal.

As I was in the Army Reserve for up to four years, I was worried that I could be called up to join them again. Despite having a job in the Pit, this did not exempt men from being called up on Reserve Duty. At the time we had a conservative government, the Prime Minister was Anthony Eden. I couldn't see a conservative government allowing the Egyptians to get away with it. When the French government started to call troops up, the English followed. On the 2nd of August, 20,000 British Reservists were called up for duty.

Unfortunately, I was called back into the Army. I had hoped that it was only a small conflict, and I would escape the call up. I went around the corner to see Jimmy. He didn't get called up. His excuse was that he had applied to emigrate to Canada. Jimmy never went to Canada.

I was called up to join the 3rd Battalion Grenadier Guards at Pirbright in early August. The day I was called up, my father came to the Deal Railway Station with Joan and my five-month-old son, Paul. It was a Sunday afternoon. I had only received the card the day before, so it was quite a shock. If I had not been married, I would have loved it. My father said I would have nothing to worry about as likely I would not even get into the Army uniform. That was not to be, I was in uniform within hours of arriving there. I suppose he was just trying to comfort my lass, who was crying a lot. When I did eventually leave Deal on the train, my father bought my lass an ice cream and he pushed the pram back to their home. Joan and Paul stayed at my parents' house in Deal for a few weeks. *Mum tells me she didn't feel safe to live by herself but was also worried about having enough money to pay the rent.*

Soon after, Joan's parents wanted her to move back into their house in Dover to look after her sisters while they went on holiday. She didn't want to go to her parent's house but was too nervous to say no. It must have been very hard for her, as she was only 19-years-old at the time.

Financially, we were going to find it hard now as the Army pay was not good. We had a few commitments including a big rent and some hire purchase payments. Neither Joan nor I ever went back to the house in Deal.

One of the first people that I met when I arrived back at the battalion was my old mate, George. Although he was not married, he didn't want to be back in the Army either. We were told that we were leaving from Southampton, but not told our destination. It was a mystery, but we had an idea that it was Egypt again. This time not on friendly terms. The Army made us have haircuts. George and I were the last as we both kept trying to dodge the barber, but were eventually caught for our turn.

At the time we were sailing to Egypt, the American Government was having talks with the English and French governments to avoid the conflict with the Egyptians. The ship we were sailing on was a migrant ship that had been turned into a troopship. We were kept quite busy again, much more than my last ship voyage as things would be different this time.

After all the talking between governments, they diverted the ship towards Malta. We were not told about the change of plans. I often thought that the Americans wanted to make friends with the Egyptians because the Russians were building Aswan Dam.

Malta

The Army wanted us to be fit when we arrived. Our feet hardly had the chance to touch the ground and settle in before they made us get to work on doing exercises. The camp was set up for us at an old runway from the last war. We were back in tents but this time we had to sleep on straw on the floor, which was very uncomfortable. There were American servicemen in Malta, but they were not very popular with the English servicemen that were already there.

Most of us felt that President Nasser could keep the Suez Canal, because many of the soldiers were reservists. Training included learning to jump off tanks. We would sing "let us join Nasser's Army" and were all only joking, of course, but it was a bit of a laugh. In fact, there was quite a bit of a rebellion, as we outnumbered the regular soldiers in the battalion. One time, the Officers tried to get us to lay a kit inspection. Only the full-time soldiers agreed to the order as we Reservists felt that we were not there to do that sort of thing.

The Officers thought they would do us all a favour by having a bingo night in the big tent. As the Officers sat in the tent waiting for us to turn up, some of the lads went along and pulled up the tent pegs, then they marched down to the Officer's quarters. I will never forget the expressions on the Officers' faces.

On boarding the bus heading to Valletta for an evening drink, someone kept ringing the bell to get the bus driver to get moving. The driver made us all get off the bus and he hit one of the soldiers with the starting handle from the bus. Later that night, there was a bit of a disturbance between the driver and a few locals. The police turned up. So, we finished up at the Police station for the night. The next day, the Sergeant Major came to get us out. Someone said to him, "We have come out here for two things, either to fight or go home". His answer was, "Well, you are fighting then. So now there will be no visiting Valletta for a few days."

In the meantime, Joan was having problems living at her parents' house. Her letters were upsetting me so much that I kept trying to get compassionate leave to fly home. I tried several times until eventually they gave me permission to go home for four weeks. The airfare back home was at my own cost. I felt that the government was a bit hasty in calling the Reservists up too soon. It also bothered me that we had given up the house in Deal, as I was just settling back into the Pit.

When I arrived at Heathrow Airport, I was the only one to be fully searched by Customs. It surprised me that I was picked on, being a serviceman. All I had was a full kit of dirty washing. I stayed in England for a few weeks and while I was there; they started to demob some of the reservists from other regiments. Despite this, they still sent me back to join the 3rd Battalion.

I arrived in Malta, but my regiment had gone on to Cyprus, so they put me into the Maltese Army Camp for a few days until they could give me transport to Cyprus.

The Colonel of the Maltese Army tried to get me to join the Maltese Army. From what I had seen of the island, Malta didn't appeal to me back then. The Army found me a ride, a Royal Air Force plane going to Cyprus. I had to sit on the floor of the plane all the way to Cyprus.

Cyprus

The British troops were in Cyprus because the Greeks and the Turks could not get on together and we had to keep the peace between the two factions. We couldn't leave the camp as neither side wanted us there. I am sure they would have loved a good punch up between us all. Whilst we were there, our role was to catch terrorists. We would surround a village to search it, usually early in the morning. Sometimes it was very embarrassing because they usually knew we were coming. Thankfully, it was not long before a ship called *The Empire Clyde* was called to take us Reservists back to Southampton. We left Cyprus in late December 1956.

We missed Christmas altogether. Worse still, the ship ran out of beer a long time before we arrived back in Southampton on New Year's Eve. Finally arriving back on home soil, we caught a train to Pirbright to be discharged from the Army. I was hoping that would be the last call up, even though I still had another three years as a Reservist to go. *Military enlistment period was three years plus four years as a Reservist. Dad felt being on call for deployments of up to seven years was too long for a family man.*

I was really looking forward to getting back to my family. This time I was returning to Dover to a place called "Victoria Dwellings". Joan had found a flat in Dover. It was a huge Victorian building consisting of approximately 40 flats. It was a nice and comfortable place inside, having a combustion stove, fueled by coal, to keep the flat warm. We had gaslights that were hard to light. It made Joan quite nervous, lighting them with a naked flamed piece of paper. The Pit delivered free coal to miners, and having too much ourselves, we were able to share with the grateful neighbours. It was here that Paul learnt to walk. He loved standing on the balcony watching the ferries come in.

I was looking forward to getting back to the Pit and bringing a wage home every week. The 9am to 5pm shift I had before was not feasible living in Dover, so I was put on the Training Coalface and the instructor was called Ned Bradford. He was 74 years of age and lived in Dover.

While living in Dover, we often put Paul in the pram and walked into town after the shops had closed. We had an imaginary black book in which we would pretend to write down what we would buy if ever we had the money. We were still thinking of the big money that I hoped to earn when I had done my coalface training, but that would be a long time off—120 days on very poor money. We would have to struggle on with it.

The last day of my coalface training was a Friday afternoon. As there were a lot of men missing that day, they were two men short to make the number up on my father's coalface. He offered my mate Brian Smith and me the chance to go on his face that day. These men were classed as the big hitters of the Pit because they always earned big money. Nervously, we both went to the coalface because it was our first time. We did what was expected of us and got paid the same wage as the men on the face the following week.

I felt that I couldn't let my father down because he oversaw the coalface. My father had kept the same men working with him that had been working with him when he had his accident. The other men in the Pit always respected him because he was fair when it came to paying their wages. If the men who worked for him worked hard, he always made sure they earned good money.

Working on the coalface was different from what it is today (1996). There was no machinery, as they have now. In those days, it was just a pick, shovel and a seven pound weighted hammer to knock up the props. We had an air pick to get the coal down, then we would have to shovel the coal onto a conveyor belt. The Charge Man would usually crawl along the face to mark out each person's stint. Each person would get equivalent to anything from eight to 10 tonnes to clear. If you were a bit unlucky by taking a long time to finish your stint, the older Colliers would not help you. At first, I found this hard, but it was not long before I could finish earlier than some of the other men on the face.

John

We started to look for a better flat in a much nicer area when Joan was expecting again. We eventually found one on Folkestone Road, Dover. Unfortunately, it was only one bedroom, but it had a lovely big room at the front. We had not been there long when our second son was born. John arrived on 27th November (1957) at 9pm. I was on afternoon shift at the Pit when someone phoned to tell me that my wife was in Buckland Hospital. It just so happened that her parents came to the flat that day. I came out of the Pit and had to walk three miles to Eastry village to catch a bus to Dover, to visit Joan in hospital. John was born three hours before Joan's 21st birthday. Paul and I went to stay in Deal with my parents while Joan was in hospital.

The new flat was too small for us all now and as we were somewhat overcrowded, so we placed ourselves on the council list for a council house. We hoped to be elevated up the list now that John had come along and the four of us had to share the same bedroom. Paul was in a cot and John was in a carrier cot.

On my way home from work each day, I visited the council offices to try and put a little bit of pressure on them for a council house. It finally worked, and we were given a new house up the Aycliffe Estate in Dover at 133 Old Folkestone Road. It was a two-bedroom house with a garden not far from Joan's parents' house.

The first job on the coalface didn't last long because it was such a long way from the Pit bottom. We couldn't earn good money as so much time was spent travelling to the face, but the money was good compared to what I had been earning. When this face finished, I was sent up to the High Seam to work for less money. As it was a fixed rate, you could work hard or have an easy shift because the money was the same all the time. I had a young family, and I wanted to earn as much as I could.

I didn't like the High Seam because we had to work in water all the time. This working condition was so bad that the Manager allowed our Deputy to book us an extra one pound each day. We needed two dirty lockers for our clothes, as we had a job to get them dry each day. We would be kneeling in water for six hours, and the water would also come out of the roof.

Eventually, I managed to get out of the High Seam to one of the jobs where you could earn good money. It meant hard work, but you were paid for what you did. The Tailgate Rip was the hardest job in the Pit. This time I wouldn't be shovelling coal, but rather I would be shovelling rock, anything between 10 to 15 tonnes each night.

The three of us working this area would usually be the first down into the Pit. There was no time to waste. We would strip off our clothes into shorts, then practically run up the gate one mile away to our place of work. We first pulled out all the support under the rip. Then we would bore about 10 or more six-foot holes. It was the role of the Deputy to come and fire the rock to the ground. We then had to shovel it all up the side of the rip (as the face was lower than the roadway, the extra height was called the rip or the ripping lip). We usually had to set two steel rings that were in two sections. For this work, we would be paid 13 pounds a yard between the three of us. We would each carry an eight pint water container. We called it a "Dudley" and would drink a lot each shift.

If we finished our work late, we would have to run down to the gate at the pit bottom. I couldn't be late because if I missed the bus back to Dover, I would have to walk three miles to catch another bus. That would really make me late home to Dover. I often slept on the bus trip home and woke up as the bus pulled into the Dover Bus Depot.

Alison Simpson

The Union had us all in the office one Friday to give us a telling off. Apparently, our job should have been a four-man job rather than three, as we had been doing it. The manager was in trouble too because of the money we were making. We told the Union if they could get a person who was prepared to work as hard as us and worked the night shift, we would take him on. Well, we didn't get anyone to come and join us.

One coalface that I worked on was so hot at night we had to put saltwater tablets into our water before going down the Pit. We would sweat so much that salt was needed to keep us well. It wasn't nice to drink, but it kept us hydrated.

I was on night shift and the big horse race, Grand National, was going to be held that day. Joan had me put two shillings and sixpence for a win on a horse called "Nickless Nickleby", a grey horse. I'm sure the only reason for choosing that horse was because it was a lovely colour. Joan watched the race on television while I was in bed, having worked the Friday night shift. Her horse won, so Joan came upstairs to wake me. We went into Dover that night to celebrate with the winnings. We had never backed a horse before.

We had no trouble in finding a willing babysitter. Often it was Joan's Aunty Margaret. We had a television, and she didn't have one, so it was quite a treat for her too. Sometimes we would just go to our favourite pubs. Joan would have a few ports and lemons and I would have a few pints of bitter. Then, we caught the last bus home.

When we first got our television, there was a weekly British science fiction programme called "Doctor Who." The episodes were produced by the British BBC TV in 1963. *"The programme depicts the adventures of a Time Lord called 'the Doctor' an extraterrestrial being who appears to be human. The Doctor explores the universe in a time-travelling space ship called the TARDIS. Its exterior appears as a blue British police box, which was a common sight in Britain in 1963 when the series first aired. With various companions, the Doctor combats foes, works to save civilisations and helps people in need." (https://en.wikipedia.org/wiki/Doctor_Who)*

Paul loved to watch it, but John often hid behind the lounge chair, just bobbing up every now and then to watch it. Maybe it was a little frightening for very young children.

I remember watching "Doctor Who" when I was about five years old in 1969. The tin foil wrapped adults, cardboard cutout scenery and the Daleks were quite scary for me. "Doctor Who" stopped production in 1989 but was relaunched in 2005 by BBC Wales TV. This time, my children were able to get involved with "Doctor Who's" galactic adventures. We never missed an episode as a family, gluing ourselves to it every week broadcasted on Australian TV. We soaked up the time travelling "Doctor Who" and his assistant on all their universal pursuits that ultimately always saved the day.

My family and I moved to England for a two-year working holiday in 2009-2010, whilst there we travelled to Wales to the set of "Doctor Who". It was very high up on our bucket list. The boys bought toy souvenirs of "Doctor Who's" Tardis and the Sonic Screwdriver, much to their delight.

In the winter on Saturday nights, Joan and I often slept downstairs on a pull-out-bed, in front of the fire. That would really confuse the boys, as they would come along hoping to stay in our bed with us. They never came down together, but not long after one came down, the other would do the same. We only allowed them to stay a few minutes, then we took them back to bed. Joan would read them another story. Storytelling always seemed to do the trick.

One morning, Paul went downstairs to make his mother a cup of tea. Unfortunately, he didn't use tea, but rather he used cocoa and water from the kitchen tap. Not only that, but he also forgot to turn the tap off, nearly flooding the kitchen.

Now that we were living in a house and not a flat, a friend of mine gave us a puppy. It was a lovely little dog, and we called him Kim. I tried to train him not to come into the front room. All was going well until he heard me go to work at 9pm. As he heard the front door close, he came trotting into the room where he was then allowed to stay until the last one went to bed.

When I came home from work, I would take Kim for a walk up the banks, behind our house, or along the cliff tops. As I had just come off night shift, I liked to sit down. When I did this, though, Kim would stand in front of me barking until I stood up and started to walk again.

When we all went for walks up the banks, we could make Kim sit down at the top of the bank until we signalled him to come. He patiently waited for the signal as we wandered on until nearly out of sight. We called him, and he would nearly fall over as he raced down the hill towards us.

One day I was having pains in the stomach, such that I decided to visit the doctor in town. He was not sure what was wrong with me and even had to ask one of the other doctors for advice. When they had decided what was wrong with me, they were really surprised that I had come down to his surgery on the bus. Nevertheless, he still sent me home to get some clothes before heading off to the hospital. I again travelled by bus. I ended up in hospital for a week to have my appendix out. Joan brought the two boys to see me, but they were not allowed into the hospital in those days. So, they would be lifted to the window, one at a time. I wanted to leave the hospital as soon as possible.

First Family Holiday

It was the Pit's holidays when I finally got out of hospital. As such, we decided to go for some sort of holiday ourselves. Joan had an Uncle Fred who had a big two-room tent, which he offered to lend us. We decided to have our first holiday at Greatstone, some 30 miles from Dover.

It was a hard place to get to and I don't really remember how we got there. We must have taken a taxi to Dover Railway Station, then a train to Ashford, then another train to Romney, and then a taxi to Greatstone. With two small boys, a big tent and all our clothes, plus cooking utensils and our dog, Kim, it must have been some effort, but we eventually got there.

We asked at the butcher's shop, in Greatstone, if we could pitch our tent behind his shop. Well, he said yes, the only problem was that despite all my efforts, I couldn't erect the tent. After a lot of difficulty, I had to give up. There was only one thing to do. I had to make my way back to Dover and get Uncle Fred to come back to help us. He was happy to come, but I had to sit on the back of his motorbike all the way back to Greatstone. In those days, there were not many people with telephones. It turned out to be a very long day before we got the tent erected.

We had permission to get water that we needed from the pub across the road using a bucket. There was not much at Greatstone, but it had a very flat sandy beach. If the tide was out, you had a long walk to get to such a depth where you could swim. At that time, Paul and John could not swim. They were quite happy to play in the sand and play with our dog, Kim. John would get very tired, so I would end up carrying him on my shoulders.

We didn't have a watch with us on holiday, so Joan would volunteer to go and ask someone. One time, she went over the sand dune to see someone cycling along. She waited until the cyclist got closer, before she walked out to ask him the time. He nearly fell off his bike, as he was blind in one eye. It must have been a bit of a shock for him in the early hours of the morning, being only 5.30am.

One of the attractions at Greatstone was the Miniature Railway. It was only 100 yards away from where we were camping. We took Paul and John to see it.

For our journey back to Dover, we took two taxis and two trains. Our next-door neighbour jokingly said we looked like gypsies getting out of the taxi. We all looked well, though, having spent a whole week in the sun. We really enjoyed our very first family holiday.

In the late summer, we would go for long walks up the banks looking for blackberries or into the fields looking for mushrooms. Sometimes we took a small stove with us so we could make a cup of tea and a bottle of water for Paul and John. We loved living close to the countryside, being just up the road with the cliffs behind us. Living in the Aycliffe Estate, there were loads of children Paul and John could play with.

One Christmas, we bought Paul a Police car that he could sit in. Paul thought that if he pulled the aerial, the car would start moving. Well, it did upset him when he had to use the pedals. Paul was about two-years-old.

Another year, I made two wooden toys for the boys. John had a farmyard and Paul had a garage. We bought farmyard animals for John and cars for Paul. Every Christmas Eve, Paul and John would hang up their stockings on the fireplace mantelpiece. The only problem being that we had to let the fire out on Christmas Eve, or they may have caught on fire. Then it became a chilly evening.

The new school year in England starts in September, after the summer holidays. We tried to get Paul into school when he was four and a half years old at Archcliffe School, just down the road from our house. We were told they didn't have the room to take Paul, much to Paul's disappointment. He cried most of the way home. He started school the following year, 1961 in February, just before his fifth birthday in March. When Paul started school, he could tell the time as we had bought him a watch for his birthday. John was never interested in learning how to tell the time. His reasoning was, "If I need to know the time, I will ask Paul". Paul had his bus fare, but he would often walk home from school so he could buy sweets for his little brother, John.

I was doing well at the Pit. The Manager had put a notice up, as they needed more deputies. The Manager called me to his office and at the time I didn't know why he wanted to see me. He asked me to go on the Deputy's course. He had already put my name down. I had to decline his offer as I was earning more money then and needed it for my young growing family. Things were not always good at the Pit because they did have a lot of strikes. That was one reason why I should have taken the Manager's offer to become a Deputy; they never went on strike.

When I look back, I might not have been much worse off financially, if I had become a Deputy. It was the same in the Army when I was recommended as a Non-Commissioned Officer. This thought would never have entered my head back then. I was having too much fun as a young lad for an Officer's role in the Army.

During one strike, while working in the bottom seam, I turned up on day shift. It was a Tuesday, and the Union called a meeting. We were all down the Pit when they told us that it would be a stay down strike. They had to do it that way, so management wouldn't have known. If management had known, they wouldn't have allowed us down the Pit. I stayed down in the Pit for four days. When I eventually came out, I looked like a ghost. I was so white, having lost the entire colour in my face.

This strike was because the Coal Board wanted to retrench 150 young haulage boys. It was terrible being down there, but we were put in a difficult position by the Union. The Coal Board made a big mistake, as all the haulage boys left the Pit. So, the Pit had to try and get some of them to come back to the Pit. The other Pits didn't have as many strikes as we did. The Coal Board was always threatening to close Betteshanger even as far back as 1956, but it turned out it was the last Pit to close in Kent. There was a stay down strike in the Pit, which lasted for six days. During this time, 120 miners lived in the Pit.

Food was usually sent down each day from the canteen where the canteen girls declared their full support for us. The Union had established complete workers' control. An unlimited supply of snuff chewing tobacco was sent down the Pit together with books, cards and dominos. I remember singing a few songs too. I expect one of those songs would have been "Keep the red flag flying high", as most of the Union in those days belonged to the Communist party.

I don't think there would have been many Union men down the Pit. They would have been in their own warm beds at night. My Uncle Jack stopped down the Pit. He was a Union man. He had worked the night before. By the end of the week, I had had enough of canteen pies, because they were cold by the time we got them. I had to wear the same clothes for the four days that I was down the Pit. The Betteshanger men eventually won their case against the sacking. The Coal Board had to back down.

The Coal Board Chairman came to the Pit as Betteshanger was going to have "Chocks" (wooden or steel movable pieces to support the cross girders to hold up the roof for safer access) on this coalface, the first in England. If any new machinery had to be tried out in any of the English Pits, Betteshanger was always the first. As the Chairman crawled along the coalface to inspect the area, he asked one of the men, "Why do you only work four days a week?" The answer was, "I couldn't manage on three". The Betteshanger men always spoke their truth regardless of who they were talking to. The Manager often had a red face from feeling embarrassed by his outspoken miners.

One time, I can remember having to walk home from the Pit following an afternoon shift. The Pit bus could not get through to Betteshanger to pick us up after our shift due to the snow. This meant I had to walk back to Dover at 10.30pm. Sometimes the bus from Dover could not get past Whitfield, on the way to Deal. That was not so bad, as we would still get paid if the bus had tried to get us to work.

We acquired a new Under Manager (second in charge after the Manager) from one of the Pits up north. He hadn't been told about the Betteshanger men and their funny ways. In typical Betteshanger style, my Uncle Jack and some men had to go and see the Under Manager in his office below ground. As they walked in wearing their Pit hats, the Under Manager told them to take their hats off. My Uncle Jack said, "We have not come in here for a haircut, we have come in here for more money". Despite this, it was not long before the new Under Manager settled in and turned out to be a good Manager. This man has now retired and lives in Deal.

When the miners came to Deal from Barnsley, they were initially met with a lot of hostility from the Deal townsfolk. I recall notices in windows of houses seeking tenants but stating "room to let—miners need not apply" or "no miners or dogs allowed". As the years passed by, the people of Deal soon got used to having miners in town as they had plenty of money to spend.

Our area General Secretary, Jack Dunn, was a self-educated man who harboured a bitter memory of the time he passed his "Eleven Plus" Exam for Grammar School. He was not able to go because his parents couldn't afford the uniform. Miner's children were lucky if they made it into Grammar School.

Going to work on the bus through the Kent countryside for an afternoon shift was a sheer test of will. The bus passed through orchards, fields and country pubs that were still serving the dinner-time drinkers. This was particularly so in summer months.

Sunday night was always the worst night of the week if you were on day shift Monday. Sunday night was often a desperate attempt to get to sleep before feeling tired, but constantly waking up throughout the night in anticipation of sleeping in the following morning. I had to be up at 4.30am for a Monday dayshift. I would be home by 3pm. It was a very long day. When I got home, I went straight to bed. I often wanted to stay there until the next morning but would get up for tea with the family.

The cages were only made for short men, five feet tall. If you were taller, you had to bend your head or crouch. One time at Betteshanger, the cage was full of men who were descending to the Pit bottom and met with some obstruction on the guide ropes halfway down. The cage stopped, but the main rope continued to unwind on to the top of the cage. Under tremendous weight, the steel cage broke free and plummeted at least 30 feet. The stationary rope then suddenly pulled it back up. The cage just jumped up and down like a Yo-Yo.

One of the men in the cage was a Jehovah's Witness. He remarked that he was not frightened of the prospect of a sudden death, because he was secure of a place in heaven. I'm sure a lot of men who went down the Pit in the cage knew that could always happen again. That's why father and son were never allowed to travel in the same cage.

Betteshanger Colliery had a unique claim; it was the most militant Pit in the British Coalfields. Its men were very proud of a continuous history of industrial action for better conditions. There was a time when the Union tried to get me to become a Union Official. It meant I would have to go to Ruskin College to study Union matters. As I would have to go away during the Pit's fortnight holiday, I declined the offer.

In the summer, Deal held a Regatta. Originally, it was always held on the days when the miners were working. This changed over time when the local council became Labour dominated. My Uncle Sid was the first Labour Councillor for Deal.

The miners built their own Welfare Clubs. I often boxed in the Deal Welfare Club when I was a young lad. These clubs promoted a sense of community for the miners to enjoy social and leisure activities. They did not want to work on Friday the 13th, it was believed to be an unlucky day.

Underground coal mining was always a high-risk job. The threat of serious injury or fatality had to be monitored. For this reason, the older experienced miners avoided where possible any potential risk, including heeding many superstitions.

The miners became more accepted in Deal, even so I decided to leave the Pit and work as a docker. Dockers could earn a good wage when there were boats to be unloaded. Joan had an uncle who worked on the docks, Uncle Fred. He was the only man that would go to work in the summer wearing a duffle coat that had big pockets. He filled the pockets with goods that fell off the back of lorries. I knew a lot of the men that worked down at the docks and they frequently used the same pub as me.

The Dockers were hard workers. In those days, there were no container ships. Everything was handled manually and would be very heavy at times. The only trouble was when one ship had been unloaded, we might have days to wait before the next one would come in to be unloaded.

I really liked the work and got on well with the men. The man that employed us called me over one day to ask if I would work with another crew, as the men that I worked with belonged to the Dockers Union. Not many of the men belonged to the Union as they classed it as casual work. We would go down in the morning when a ship was due. There would be as many as 50 men hoping to get a job with only 30 jobs available. I was always lucky and got a job.

Someone reported me to the Miners' Union saying that I was working down at the Docks in Dover. My father was so worried he must have caught the next bus to Dover to find out what was happening. I guess someone was trying to get me into trouble. It didn't work, as I had done everything above board. I had finished at the Pit and worked out my notice officially.

I loved the work that I was doing, being out in all kinds of weather in good fresh air, as opposed to underground darkness in the Pit. One thing particularly good was being home every night. I was now getting colour back into my face. However, I wasn't working every day. Some days we would just hang about in a cafe drinking cups of tea. One cup of tea would last for hours. A lot of these men had always done this type of work. I didn't like hanging around waiting for work. As much as I liked the work, I felt I had to go back to the Pit. I was told all I had to do was to phone the Pit and there would be a job for me.

So, I went back to the Pit. My job at the docks was only for the summer months. My shifts at the Pit were days and afternoon shifts. Now we could fill the coal bunker at home with coal. Joan and I realised that it was nice to have a big fire in the winter. We had a back boiler behind the fire that would heat the water. Christmas was on the way, so we enjoyed buying lots of presents for the boys as they still believed in Father Christmas.

We booked a holiday to Ostend in Belgium. It was exciting going to another country. Paul was five and John was nearly four. Our only problem was we now had a dog, Kim, that we could not take with us. Kim was always with us wherever we went. Paul and John's grandparents, who lived in the Ropewalk, said they would look after

Kim, providing he stayed in the shed in the back garden. At the time, we were a little upset that Kim would have to be an outside dog, as we let him come inside our house to the kitchen. As it turned out, however, this was not to be. The night before we were due to go on holiday, we gave Kim a good bath to make him look nice and clean.

On the day of the holiday, Kim managed to get out of the garden by jumping over the back fence. We didn't know at the time until someone knocked at the front door only to be told that a bus had run over and killed our dog. We were all very upset knowing that we were going on holiday but couldn't do anything at the time as we had booked and paid for our holiday. I had the unpleasant task of burying Kim up the road. I took him to where we would often take him for a walk. We couldn't help feeling that our dog knew we were going to leave him.

One of our neighbours drove us to the docks to catch the ferry to Ostend. We stayed at a guesthouse for a week. It included bed, breakfast and an evening meal. Breakfast we found different; it was a continental breakfast. At home, we always had a cooked breakfast. We did have a nice holiday despite not having a lot of money to spend, along with our deep sadness of losing Kim. We had a day trip across the border to Holland from Belgium, where John got to have his photo taken with a Dutch lady who was selling fruit from a street wheelbarrow. She was wearing the national dress, but Paul refused to have his photo taken, as we think he was still upset over the death of Kim.

Back home, I managed to get myself a motorbike. It was a green BSA 250cc English motorbike. The bike was big and heavy compared to today's standards. I managed to ride it home from the shop. One of our next-door neighbours offered to show me how to ride it. He came out to show me and stood there explaining what to do, but before he had finished telling me, I shot off up the road on the bike. I can say I was quite worried and was not the only one concerned. Lucky for me, it was a quiet road. I didn't keep the motorbike long. One day, I had an accident coming down Castle hill having skidded on some gravel. The council had put it down because of the snow.

The bike fell on top of me. I had to lie there until someone in a car stopped to lift the bike off me. I decided not to keep the bike and took it back to the shop. In those days, it was not compulsory to wear safety helmets. I was lucky, there wasn't much traffic behind me on the hill. That was the end of motorbikes for me.

We would often go to Deal by train to see my parents, as it was much quicker than a bus, and they lived close to the train station. Travelling by bus was slower but enjoyable as we watched the countryside go by. The bus would take us through St Margaret's Bay, which was a very posh village. We never thought that one day we would be living there.

My eldest brother, Douglas, was married to June and now it was my sister's turn. Sonia married a British Royal Marine, Jim. We bought smart new clothes for Paul and John to wear, especially for Sonia's wedding. A happy family occasion.

In 1963, we had an interview at Australia House in London to emigrate to Australia. A few months later, we received a letter saying we could go within a fortnight. Australia House had booked a flight for us to fly to Australia the following fortnight. We were so nervous that we had to phone Australia House and cancel it. Joan and I were only 26 and 29 and frightened to take the plunge at such short notice with our little boys, who were only four and six.

Alison

Alison was born at 10pm on Sunday 16th February (1964) in a private maternity home (hospital) at Kearsney Abbey, Dover. The building was a 17th century manor house with its own chapel on seven acres of parkland, including its own lake. *Mum tells me the parkland gardens had lots of squirrels in the trees and ducks on the lake. It was run by French Catholic Nursing Nuns who would chatter amongst themselves in their French language.*

It was very unusual in those days for working-class people (miners) to have their children born in a private nursing home. We had to save a lot of money. We also got help from the government. Many people spent the government issued money on clothes and such things as prams or cots. We had to get most things all over again as Paul and John were now six and seven years old, but we were able to save well. Children were not allowed in nursing homes or hospitals in those days. So, when I went along to visit Joan and baby Alison, Paul and John stood in the garden and looked up to the top window to see their mother. I took some chocolates for Joan, and she would throw them down to Paul and John as little gifts. At the time, it was hard for Joan, as she could not cuddle her boys, only wave from the window to them.

We settled into our two-bedroom house in the Aycliffe Estate at 111 Old Folkestone Road and did not want to leave the area, because the boys had made lots of friends. Alison was eight months at the time. She slept in our bedroom, as we did not want her to wake the boys at night. We approached the council to see if they would let us have a three-bedroom council house now that we had a baby girl. Before they would give us a three-bedroom house, the council had to send someone to inspect the house that we were already living in. We must have passed the inspection well, as it was not long before the council offered us a three-bedroom house a little way down the road in the same street.

We went down the road to inspect the new house we were offered. When we took Alison into the empty house, she immediately burst into tears. As soon as we moved in, I painted the ceiling in the front room. It took several coats of white paint before I could get it looking white again. We were lucky to get a house so quickly. Most people had to wait years. Getting a house just down the road helped a lot, as we loved this area and were comfortably settled.

It was very exciting moving into a bigger house. The first thing we wanted to do was to buy new fitted carpet. We bought Axminster carpet, being one of the best carpets that you could buy at that time. It had a lovely pattern on it and covered the front room floor. It took us a long time to pay it off. We had a lovely dining room suite and therefore the room looked nice.

This house had a bigger garden and had been well looked after by the people who lived there before us. They were obviously keener on gardening than I was at the time. It even had a vegetable patch with some cabbages still growing that had been left for us.

The boys still had to share a bedroom, but Alison now had her own room. At the back door, this house had a much larger coal bunker, so we could now have our full quota of coal delivered. In our previous house, the coal bunker was too small, enabling the coal man to sell a few extra bags of coal.

Some Sundays I would take Paul and John over the hills for a countryside morning walk, then call into the pub for a shandy and a packet of crisps for the boys before getting home to Joan's roast Sunday dinner. The smell wafting down the streets every Sunday was grand, as most families cooked this traditional roasted meal each week.

The roasted meat was often beef, lamb, pork or chicken. This tradition started back in the 15th Century where the "Beefeaters" (Yeomen of the Guard, who were the royal bodyguards) used to eat a lot of roasted beef, hence their nickname "The Beefeaters". Yorkshire pudding is a floured batter (plain flour, egg, milk, salt) that is whisked into a batter then roasted in the oven. The poorer community could not afford to buy a lot of meat so they would fill up on Yorkshire pudding and gravy as their entree. Now the Yorkshire puddings are much smaller and served with the main course. Some pubs in England still serve their Yorkshire puddings very large, dinner plate size, with the meat, potatoes, gravy and vegetables on top. This would be my dad's favourite meal of the week.

Although I loved living on Old Folkestone Road, there was a lot of trouble in the Kent Pits. At Betteshanger we had a lot of strikes, we never seemed to get a good period of work. Many men were leaving and joining the Cross Channel boats. Those jobs were not permanent jobs, but there was always a chance they could be kept on. Sometimes the men in those jobs would have to go on other ships that were away for much longer trips.

One of the reasons why the Betteshanger men were so militant was the fact they were sent from Barnsley, Yorkshire to Kent between the two world wars. The government threatened to withdraw their unemployment benefit if they did not move to Kent for coal mining.

The men that did leave the Pit to go on the Cross Channel ferries would most likely go on the Townsend Ferries as cooks or waiters; a far cry from working down the coal mine. Funnily, there were so many men working for the Townsend Ferries, they were nicknamed "The Betteshanger Ferries". Seems crazy being a coal miner one day to a waiter or cook the next. The incentive could have been the duty-free cheap drink and cheap cigarettes that you could get off the boats.

The Pit Manager made me a Charge Man. I was now in charge of 28 men. This meant I would put them in the jobs on the face that I thought most suitable to them. It was not a popular job, as you couldn't please everyone. I was paid five shillings a day extra. I often felt the extra money was not enough reward for the extra responsibility. Being a Charge Man also meant that I often had to attend Saturday morning meetings, even after a Friday night shift. If it wasn't for the Cornish pasties and a bottle of beer, I am sure I would have slept through the meetings. These meetings were designed to help come up with ways to increase production. After the meeting, I would have 1.7 miles walk back to Eastry to catch a bus home to Dover.

With the advent of mechanised coal extraction, the era of the Big Hitters followed, who earned a lot of money on the front and tailgate rips. That was one reason why I didn't want to become a Deputy. I was classified as one of the Big Hitters. There was a lot of jealousy with the wages that we were earning.

Earning big money was not going to last as the Coal Board wanted to bring in the National Power Loading Agreement. This was to ensure that all workers earned the same wage, no matter what part of the Pit you worked in. Whilst some thought this was fair, the fact was that the work on the rip was much harder than on the face. The Union wanted the entire Pit to be on the same money.

It was our last week of piecework (getting paid for coal extracted) before the new agreement came in. I was a Charge Man and required to organise with the Deputy for the advance (wage) of the face length that week. The Deputy gave me the tape measure to accurately record the distance we had worked. To add some extra length, I secretly wrapped the tape measure around my arm so we could earn more money that week. Maybe I shouldn't have done that, but it was our last big wage without doing overtime. In those days, prior to the new agreement, "overtime" was a dirty word in the Pit.

Piecework finished in the Pit. One week I was on seven pounds per shift, then when the new agreement came in, I was on 84 shillings a shift. That was a big drop in wages and took away the incentive to work as hard as we were used to.

The Pit did not seem the same once the National Power Loading Agreement came in on the 6th of June 1966. The agreement guaranteed a fixed shift wage, irrespective of the amount of coal that was produced. This was the beginning of phasing out piece rates and contracts. The only good thing was that you could be sure the coalface was at least 23 inches thick, as the machine that cuts the coal would cut the face to a 23 inches height. Betteshanger was one of the most mechanised Pits in the country.

I remember the days that I had to crawl along the coalface scraping my stomach, shuffling along, to then roll onto my side so I could knock out the props. Then to continually drag myself further up the face on my stomach because the ceiling was so low. I used a seven-pound hammer that had part of the handle cut off to give me more room to swing the hammer. At the end of the shift, my stomach would be red raw from all that dragging over the ragged surfaces. All that for 98 shillings a shift (AUD$10) and that was the best paid job in the Pit. The coalface was usually 300 yards long. Those days were finished.

One night shift, I had done a lot of crawling up and down the coalface on my knees and my knee came up like a balloon. When I got home that morning, I found it increasingly difficult to walk. I went to bed thinking that it would go down after a rest. Not so. We sent for the doctor. I was told that I needed to take two weeks off and do a lot of walking. From then on, I took the boys for lots of walks out into the countryside, that was just up the road. We would often go looking for mushrooms in the fields.

I was beginning to think it was time for a change from the Pit, again. My reasoning was mainly because if they closed the Pit, there would be a lot of men looking for work and there wasn't much work in Dover or Deal. So, I thought getting out while I could find a job was the best way to do it. I was also fed up with all the shift work. In those days, we worked three different shifts on a rotation.

I joined the Townsend Ferries as a wine waiter. I was working with a student, because students would often work in the summer months to earn a little cash. There were two of us that had to keep the passengers happy with drinks in the dining room. To give me courage to serve the passengers, I would have a pint of beer down in the crew's quarters before starting my job. My mate needed more Dutch courage than I did, and I would have to go and get him, as I couldn't keep up with the drink orders. I'm sure there were a lot of customers who would walk out of the dining room when the ship docked, not having had a drink with their meal.

My mate cycled to work. I often wondered how he made it back to his tent that he and his friend lived in behind the pub, just out of Dover. One time he came to work with a big bruise on his face. He had fallen off his bike as he had cycled between the tramlines that were along the seafront of Dover.

The availability to drink was too easy on the Cross Channel Ferries. One time I got a drink for the cooks, but so that no one would see me take the drinks to them, I hurried along the deck. As I hurried along with the drinks, there was a man sitting there enjoying reading the paper. Just as I reached him, a gust of wind blew his paper down and the froth off the beer flew into his face. I did not have the nerve to stop and apologise to him.

We would do two crossings to Calais, France, every night on a 12-hour shift. I didn't like the job. I was now working longer hours and would do a 48-hour week. I couldn't wait for the season to finish, as I knew I would get a job back at the Pit.

Incredibly, I bumped into a student that I had worked with on the boat some 25 years later in Trafalgar Square, London. He and his friend had established an English school in Paris. He said that they had only been talking about me the day before. I must have left an impression on them to be talking about me 25 years later.

After the season finished, I went back to the Pit. I am sure I was only meant to be a miner. The concession of coal was always a good incentive to go back to the Pit. I wouldn't have known the full price of coal. We used coal to heat our homes. I went back to Betteshanger Pit as if I'd just had a long holiday.

We loved our house. Alison began walking all over the place. We were proud of our garden too. Alison loved eating coal though, she would head to the coal bunker and help herself. Our next-door neighbour would often call out that Alison was in the coal bunker again. Maybe she was teething because she also liked biting the paint off the side of her cot. The cot got so bad I took it into the back garden to strip the paint off in order to repaint it, but I was not able to strip the paint in time before she was due for a bed. At 18-months-old, she started sleeping in a bed, never to return to the cot.

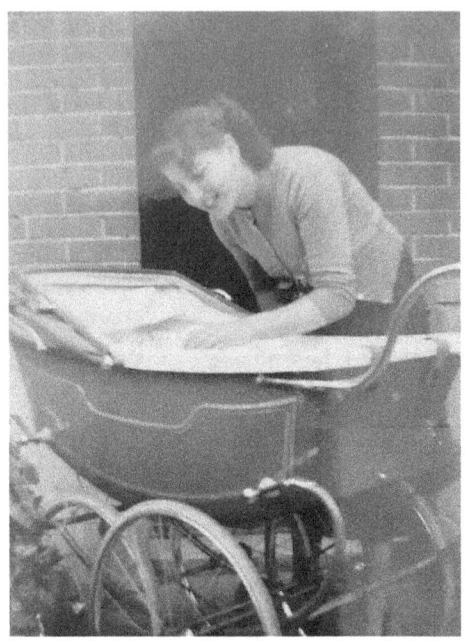

Paul in pram with Joan.

Joan holding Paul, wearing her Egyptian drop earings.

Paul on Toy Bull with Arnold and pregnant Joan.

Arnold holding baby Alison with John on steps.

Alison Simpson

John and Kim (dog) at the beach.

8
ITCHY FEET

Yorkshire (1965)

There was an advertisement for people to move to Leeds. The council was building lots of new houses and seeking expressions of interest. My brother, Douglas, had recently been demobbed from serving in the Royal Air Force and was living in Leeds with his new wife, June, and their daughter, Suzanne. We decided to apply and after a short wait we were offered a council house in Leeds, on a new estate called Manor Farm. One of the reasons we were able to get the house in Leeds was because the council had trouble getting people to pay big rents. It was a lovely three-bedroom house with under floor heating that we had never had before. We only had a fireplace.

When we agreed to the new house in Manor Farm, one of the first things we did was to buy a new stove in Dover and have it delivered to the house in Leeds by the Leeds Electricity Board. Upon arriving at our new home, the stove was there. It was the best stove available at that time. We would set the stove on before going to bed as it had a fan that would flow up the stairs and it was always warm when we got up in the morning. We took all our furniture with us to Leeds, even our lovely, fitted carpet.

Paul and John went to the same school, Belle Island Primary. They were always smartly dressed in their uniforms. Paul was soon made a School Prefect, and both Paul and John made new friends.

Swimming baths were everywhere. To us, they seemed to be on every corner. Paul and John learned to swim living here. We would go to the swimming baths sometimes twice a day, once in the morning before school and then again after teatime at night.

Joan's Uncle, John Chase, took Paul to see his first live football match, seeing the local lads, Leeds United, play. Paul enjoyed it so much that we often went together to watch a game. We would come home to pork pies and tinned tomatoes for teatime. I think both Paul and John enjoyed living in Leeds.

The boys joined a club that was run by the church, hoping that they might choose to go to church. We never made them go to church, as they didn't have that interest. We lived a few doors from a lovely park. Leeds was well known for its beautiful parks. We often went to our local park to play football, tennis or sometimes a game of cricket. In the park at summertime, there was a tearoom selling tea and cakes. We found Leeds to have lovely shops, too.

I managed to get a job coal mining at Middleton Broom Pit. First, they had to find out if I was experienced enough to work at the face. It didn't take them long to see that I was fully equipped to be working there.

As a new starter, I had to go onto night shift, but it didn't pay any extra money. They put me with a crew that went around the Pit finishing off what the previous shift did not complete. After a few weeks, I found out that we were not getting paid the same rate as the other shifts. We were getting 55 shillings a shift, but the other shifts were getting 65 shillings a shift. After a discussion with the rest of the crew, they made me spokesman to go over at the end of the night shift and put our case to the Under Manager.

On our way, we met the Manager crossing the Pit yard. He stopped me to say that he had heard good things about me. He did not know at the time we were on our way to see the Under Manager about our pay of which I knew we were entitled to. He wouldn't have said that to me if he'd known what we were up to. We arrived at the Under Manager's office and he gave me a funny look; it was left up to me to do the talking. When I'd finished talking, he asked me who I was. We left the office having won the case, but the Under Manager took me off this shift and put me on a job that only paid 45 shillings a shift.

I found the Yorkshire miners to be frightened of their own shadows. After working in Betteshanger, I soon realised the Yorkshire miners were very different. One good thing was that I now only had a 10-minute walk to the Pit each day.

The men on the night shift wanted me to stand for the Union, but I declined because the only men that knew me were those who worked on the night shift. The Under Manager made sure I was kept away from the face the rest of the time I was there. It was not long before I broke my wrist, so I was off work for a few weeks.

At this time, John recalls being only seven-years-old, when he went to visit his Grandma Hinchcliffe (Dad's mother) but she wasn't home. His Uncle David, 12-years- old, was. The television was broadcasting the state funeral of Sir Winston Churchill (January 1965). David got a packet of chocolate biscuits out from the cupboard to share with John. They ate the entire packet between them as they watched the funeral procession on TV. When Grandma Hinchcliffe got home to find the packet had been demolished, she wasn't too pleased, according to John's recollection.

The possibility of high electric bills always worried us, though. Having lived in Kent, we were already accustomed to paying high rent for a council house. We never turned on our under-floor heating because our neighbours warned us of the high electric bills we would get. I didn't realise at the time that because I wasn't getting my coal allowance, I would have been entitled to an allowance for our electricity bills instead. The only time we ever turned on our under-floor heating was the day we left the house, just to see what it was like. It felt marvellous, having it on only for a few hours.

Alison Simpson

We were in Leeds when England won the World Football Cup on the 30th of July 1966. At that time, my father had come to visit us. We were lucky, as he would never travel very far. I took him to the local pub on Sunday, the following day. Pubs did not open until noon, closing at 2pm on Sundays. There were always a lot of men waiting for opening time. Usually there would be about 50 men standing out on the Green in front of the pub waiting for the doors to open. So, then it would be a rush to get served. As I was not a regular, I had a job to get served.

Joan and I were convinced by Douglas and June to move in with them, so we could save to buy our own house. We gave up our council house at Manor Farm and moved into their house at Kirkstall. Douglas was not working at the time, as he had just come out of the Royal Air Force. I talked him into going into the Pits and he successfully arranged to get on a Manager's course in Doncaster. This meant he had a lot of studying to do at Doncaster College. Douglas was the apple of my dad's eye, even more so now he was studying to be a Pit Manager.

I put my foot into it one day because I said Douglas would never make a Manager. I thought that a Manager should have to work from the shop floor, as a labourer, and climb the ladder. Douglas' wife, June, said that they were middle class and that we, Joan and I, would always be working class. I am extremely proud to be a working-class man to this day. The long hours of physical work were rewarding because I knew it was for my growing little family, who I loved very much.

In the 1960s, the social class structure was still evident in England. Some historians suggest there were five social class levels: lower class, working class, middle class, upper class and aristocrats. The level was dependent upon job or income and often repeated through the generations unless a child decided to do something different to their parents. Working in England from 2009 to 2010, I found the social class system was still alive, but being an Aussie chick, I unknowingly broke many of their rules at my workplace.

I managed to find work at a Pit nearer to Kirkstall at Lofthouse. It took two buses to get there. They put me on the afternoon shift, as I was new. The only time I got on the coalface was when they were short of men. Usually it was Mondays, as a lot of men liked to have a night out on Sundays. Occasionally, I would get Fridays.

One Friday, I caused a few ripples because they did not find me a job on the face, despite being short of men. I decided to go out of the Pit, a one-man sort of strike. But when I got to the Pit top, the Union delegate was waiting for me. He wanted me to go and see the Under Manager. I am sure they thought there could be a strike. After a lot of discussion, I went back down the Pit and from then on; I was always given a good job.

Joan often looked after Suzanne while June was at work. After school, both John and Suzanne fought with each other, trying to push the other out of the way as they scrambled up the stairs, aiming to be the first to use the toilet. We stored our furniture in Douglas' garage, not the best place, especially during the winter months.

Living with my brother and his family was simply not working out. Joan desperately wanted to get back to Dover. After three months, we realised Kent was our next move. We loved the Leeds lifestyle. Who knows, we may have stayed in Leeds if we had kept the house at Manor Farm.

The decision was made, so we packed our bags. I was certainly looking forward to working at Betteshanger Pit with the familiar crew. Our only disappointment at leaving Leeds was the boys having to change schools again.

Kent (1967)

Initially, we moved in with Joan's sister, Joy, and her family while we looked for our own flat. We soon found a flat on the outskirts of Dover in Priory Road. The best thing was that I got a job back at Betteshanger Pit with men that I really enjoyed working with.

One day, I read in the local paper that new bungalows were being built at St Margarets-at-Cliffe. I went to make some enquiries and found that we did not need such a big deposit, which was good seeing we had spent so much money moving. We decided to proceed with it. Living in the country really appealed to Joan and I. It was a particularly attractive location, as it was halfway between Deal and Dover.

Being winter, the bungalow seemed to take a long time to build. Many a weekend we would catch a bus to St Margaret's from Dover, then walk from the village to Little Acre, the name we gave our house, with Alison in her pushchair, only to find that no work had been done since our last visit. This was very disappointing, having walked that far, about one mile, in the cold weather one direction, then having to turn around and walk one mile back to the village for a bus home.

"You can see the sea from one of the windows," the builder told us. He was right, but you needed to stand on your tippy toes. We were allowed to choose our own colours for the floor and the bathroom suite. We chose green for the bathroom with dark tiles on the floor and very pale yellow for the walls.

It was 1968 when we finally moved into our newly built home on Nelson Park Road. We immediately commissioned a 14-foot fireplace wall. It was built from Yorkshire stones and black tiles for the mantlepiece. We were very proud of this modern fireplace. We installed central heating straight away, so we were never cold in the winter. We chose a new dark green telephone. Alison often ran down the hallway, fighting off Paul and John to answer the telephone first. It was sometimes her best friend, Victoria, who lived down near the farms in our area. We had a wooden plaque put on the external wall naming our new home "Little Acre". Well over 50 years later, the bungalow still wears the name we gave that home.

This is where I started to make my childhood memories. We all loved this house and our neighbourhood surrounded by the beautiful English countryside. As soon as we had moved in, Mum, discreetly standing on the other side of the fence, overheard me formally introducing my family to the neighbour in her garden. "I have a brother called John, another brother called Paul, a Daddy called Arnold, and a Mummy called Mum".

Now that we had a new house, we needed some new furniture. We chose a new dining room suite that was made of teakwood. At that time, it was an expensive wood. We bought it at a shop in Deal called "Jobs". The shop was noted for good quality furniture. I had to go to the shop every Saturday to pay some money for it. One day, I noticed that they had a children's area where they had some lovely girls' dresses. I couldn't help admiring them. An assistant said I could take three dresses home that I liked and let my little lass choose which one she liked. We bought all three dresses.

My mates at the Pit thought I should be renting, as three pounds a week was a lot to pay on the mortgage. Most of the lads at the Pit lived in houses in Mill Road, paying only 30 shillings a week.

Paul got into Dover Boys Grammar School. He had such good marks, I believe he should have gone without me having to go and see his headmaster at Castlemount Secondary School. The headmaster agreed and allowed him to go to the Grammar School. Moving to St Margaret's, Paul could continue with that school because we were still in the catchment area for his secondary schooling.

John and Alison went to the Old School in Kingsdown Road, St Margarets-at-cliffe, a long but walkable distance from our new home. John went to this school for his last year of primary school, and it was Alison's first year of school. The headmaster at this school was my teacher in Deal when I was a young lad.

Alison was not too impressed on her first day. She did a lot of crying, clinging on to her mum's leg. Her teacher, Mrs Scott, was very firm, having to physically drag Alison into the classroom, then swiftly closing the classroom door.

I do remember my first day of school and the crying match with Mum, unable to detach from her. Yes, Mrs Scott, my teacher, did drag me into the classroom, literally by the armpits, promptly closing the big wooden door behind us. She then asked an older boy to sit next to me. He was able to distract my attention by helping me draw numbers. He taught me to draw a number eight without taking the pencil off the page, as I only knew how to draw two circles. Mum felt upset all day, needlessly.

It did take a few days for Alison to realise she had to go to school every day. Alison was at the same school as John but finished her day a little earlier. She would stand in front of John's classroom wooden door, jumping up to the little window high up in the door, trying to look for John. The teacher always let Alison into John's classroom until it was time for all the children to go home.

The Old Primary School was built in 1847 and closed during World War II. The school reopened after the war but finally closed for good in 1970 when the new primary school was built on Sea Street in St Margarets-at-Cliffe.

We had settled into our new home and while the children were at school during the day, my lass was able to get a job in the local nursing home. I was on night shift so she could work day shifts. I was always home when the children came home from school.

Mum was a stay-at-home mother ever since she was 19-years old. Twelve years later, at 31-years-old, with her youngest child at school, me, she felt it was time to earn an income so they could save for more luxuries. By the late 1960s, many men started to help around the house caring for their children and doing household chores so women could work.

One Christmas we couldn't get a tree. We decided to go into the local woods to get something that resembled a Christmas tree. In those days, they didn't have artificial Christmas trees. We found a lovely big pine tree, cut it down and dragged it home through the snow. When we got it home, it was too tall, having to bend it to get it through the back sliding doors. *I vividly remember traipsing through the deep snow into the woods with Paul, John and Dad in search of the perfect Christmas tree. It was tiring for my little legs and very cold. Mum and Dad were proud of their home and loved the country lifestyle. We all have very happy memories of this home loving the countryside location. Winter snow often piled up high at our back door, and we would have to leave a spade at the door to dig ourselves out.*

Guy Fawkes night was great fun in our new neighbourhood. We joined other neighbours and built a large community bonfire. There were toffee apples for everyone, and we put potatoes under the bottom of the bonfire to cook. We had lots of fun eating, chatting and enjoying the fireworks together.

The entire neighbourhood of St Margarets-at-Cliffe, gathered in an empty field that seemed enormous to a four-year-old, where they built a massive bonfire. A neighbour opposite the bonfire opened her garage door and sold oxtail soup in little cups and slices of coconut ice. There were crowds of children. It was a lot of fun being out at night around the huge bonfire.

Paul, John and I used to wait at the end of Nelson's Road, very early on Saturday mornings, to hitch a ride on the Lorry that was delivering empty milk churns down to the dairy farm, a few miles away. It saved our legs in at least one direction. We would walk back at the end of the day, having spent the entire day at the dairy farm helping or playing with our friends that lived nearby.

I was the only coal miner living in the area. I am sure the man that delivered my coal was not too impressed having to travel so far just for me. I would often give coal to a pensioner who lived across the road from us.

This pensioner, who lived across the road from our "Little Acre" house, was always working in his shed building things. I often visited him and had many lovely chats. He was the first person to point out to my parents that I had a "lazy eye". My parents felt quite insulted at his comment, thinking that there was nothing wrong with my eyes. It wasn't until I was eight that my parents discovered I needed glasses. At age 12, I wore a patch over my lazy eye, hoping to correct it naturally, but to no avail. My left eye is completely blind and I cannot read anything from it, and my right eye has had to pick up the slack and work very hard for me throughout my entire life.

There were some lovely walks in the area, and we would often go over the fields to the top of the cliffs, then go down to the beach. On the top of the cliffs, there was a monument in memory of the men from World War I and World War II. On a clear day, you could see the coast of France and sitting there, you could watch the ferries crossing the English Channel.

Walking along the cliff tops to Deal you would have to pass through Kingsdown, which was a small village. A little further along was Walmer Castle before arriving in Deal. We loved living at St Margaret's, as we went on many long walks in the countryside in all directions.

I caught two buses to get to Betteshanger Pit. The first bus took me to Deal Castle, then I would call in to see my parents in the morning before catching a second bus to the Pit. My father and I sat in the kitchen talking Pit over a cup of tea. My dad had finished at the Pit. He was not retired, but the Coal Board wanted some men to take early retirement. I think he had just over a year to go. With the two bus rides and calling in to see my father, some days I was away from home for up to 12 hours.

It was about this time that my sister, Sonia, and her family arrived home to England after being posted to Singapore for military service. My brother-in-law, Jim, had just got demobbed from serving in the Royal British Navy. They planned to move to Wakefield, Yorkshire. With Douglas and his family already in Leeds, my mother wanted to move as well.

My parents had a lovely guesthouse in Deal called *Chez Nous* and did quite well in the summer months with holidaymakers from abroad. Some of the guests came back each year. Even though my dad worked in the Pit most of his life, the local Employment Office Labour Exchange made sure he got a job, a job that younger people wouldn't do. At 64 years of age, they gave him a job at the local Firework Factory, sweeping floors.

As far as going to live in Yorkshire, I knew my father didn't want to go. He was looking forward to the day that he could take the dog for walks along the seafront. I'm sure he looked forward to me calling in and having a chat over a cup of tea and talking Pit with him. It wasn't long before my parents had their house up for sale.

My mother thought they would not be able to take Peppe, their dog, on the train to Yorkshire, so they wanted us to take Peppe. They were really pleased that we took him because they knew he would be all right with us as we did a lot of countryside walking. Originally, my parents bought Peppe for Sonia's birthday, but soon after she was married she moved to Singapore for her husband's British Navy posting.

We loved having Peppe, a good excuse to go for long walks in search of mushrooms for breakfast. Usually mushrooms were out in autumn, from September to October. One Saturday, I took Peppe over the fields to Deal, that being at least a four-mile walk. Well, Peppe being only a small dog, got very tired. So, by the time I got to Deal, I called into a pub on the seafront to get a shandy and the poor dog just flopped down under a table outside of the pub. As my parents hadn't moved to Yorkshire yet, we went to visit them but decided to catch a bus home with Peppe. They sold their guesthouse and went to live in Wakefield, taking my brother, David, who still lived at home, with them. David would have been about 16 or 17-years-old.

I had two accidents at the Pit not long after moving into our new house at St Margaret's. The first one was on a Sunday night when I was assisting the fitter, doing maintenance on the shearer (a machine to cut coal on a longwall face). My regular job was to drive the shearer during the week. That night we had to jack the shearer up to change what was called "shoes". I had my right hand under the shearer when it fell off the jack. It cut a 1.5 inch gap in my right thumb. I was taken to Dover Hospital, staying there for a few weeks to recover.

The second accident occurred when I was breaking a big lump of stone that had fallen from the roof onto the conveyor belt. A piece of stone hit me in the eye, and I was not able to see for a while. There were no safety glasses back then. I was taken to Dover Eye Hospital where the specialist said I was lucky that I did not lose the sight in my right eye. The specialist advised me to be off work for a few weeks.

One week my lass played the Saturday Football Pools. You had to pick eight draws on your coupon to win a lot of money. Well, my lass got six numbers that she knew about, but as I had worked Friday night, I had been in bed. So, I thought I would go over to Deal on the bus to get an evening paper to check them. To our surprise, my lass got seven numbers. That meant we would get a prize, but not the big one as that week there were 11 draws on the coupon. My lass won 120 pounds (AUD$215). We were then paying 12 pounds a month mortgage, so it was a lot of money. We let Paul and John go and buy themselves a new record each.

With my lass working and me always being on night shifts, we didn't get much time off to explore this beautiful part of England. I would sometimes have a walk up to the village, usually on Sunday night, to have a pint at the Red Lion Pub. There are parts of the village that we never saw when we lived there but have since found when we go back for our holiday visits.

***

This is where Dad ended the narration of his story with Paul.

Yorkshire (1970)

All of Dad's immediate family were now living in Yorkshire, so he really wanted to follow them. He had a close relationship with his parents, especially his father. Dad was never one to let the grass grow under his feet. Some may call that "itchy feet", always up for a new adventure.

I was six, John 12 and Paul 14. As children, we had no say in the matter. Selling our first family home, "Little Acre" was difficult, but the promise of an adventure to a Yorkshire lifestyle was enticing for us all. Dad knew the houses in Yorkshire were much cheaper to buy than in Kent, so after selling our house, we would have been able to afford a very nice house up north.

Dad bought a three-bedroom semi-detached house on Woolgreaves Drive, the outer suburbs of Wakefield. It was a good street, located in a rural area, surrounded by farms. Dad loved taking us to Newmillerdam on Sundays, followed by a pub lunch or a drink in a beer garden. He made sure we all learnt to swim. I learnt to swim in the Wakefield Swimming Baths. Our entire family loved going to the Baths. It was absolute heaven for him being back in Yorkshire, where he grew up as a young boy, being able to re-live his old stomping grounds and hearing the familiar Yorkshire accents.

Dad got a job at Walton Colliery easily, and Mum found work at Sandal Grange Nursing Home. Between Mum and Dad's opposing shifts, they were able to commute respectively to their workplaces using one bicycle. Dad arrived home and passed the bike over to Mum and vice versa upon her return from work. Thanks to John's tremendous attention to detail, he can even remember the colour of this bike. It was a red ladies' bike.

Both the Walton Colliery and Lofthouse Colliery were re-purposed in the 1980s after the mining industry shut down in England. They were turned into beautiful Nature Reserve Parks for all to visit and enjoy.

Paul went to Thornes Park Secondary School. He had his final two years of school in Wakefield to complete his O levels. He walked a long way to school so he could save his bus fare money.

John went to Kettlethorpe City High, where he made a lifelong friendship with Garry Johnson. Both John and Garry loved their music. One Christmas morning, Garry proudly carried his massive new boom box on his shoulder with music blaring out loudly as he walked up our street to visit John.

John learnt to play Rugby Union at school and played on Saturday mornings. At school, John had to do sewing classes for a term, so he made me a dress. He remembers proudly getting a house point for it. My brothers were so kind to me; being the youngest sibling had its merits. It was around this time that I pestered Mum into having another baby. I would have loved an addition to our family.

I learnt to swim, ride a bike and made great friends in our neighbourhood. It was a very friendly area to live, and all the kids played together in large groups, from young ones to older ones. It felt natural to all hang out together in big groups, where the older kids looked out for the younger ones.

I went to Kettlethorpe Primary School. In the lead up to Christmas, Mum was knitting baby clothes, so I often quizzed her, hoping we were having another baby. No, the clothes were for my Baby Tears doll for Christmas, so I could play Mummy too. Paul, John, and I received so many presents from Father Christmas that year. As I look back now, their wages must have been good.

Between the ages of six to eight, I often role-played, as kids do. Some days, I would be the student in a classroom, where one of the older kids in our group would act as the teacher. We all sat behind desks in her garage while she asked us to write and learn. Other days, I would dress up as an astronaut, where Mum let me wrap myself up in silver foil and go out in the evening to my friend's house. Sometimes my friend and I would dress up as Nuns, doing the sign of the cross at all the doorways and kneeling a lot. I think the television show "The Flying Nun" was our inspiration. I also loved playing with my Baby Tears doll, role playing motherhood.

One of my friends lived in a mansion up the end of the road. They had an indoor swimming pool in a glassed conservatory surrounded by a huge walled garden, manicured by their gardener. We loved swimming in her pool. It was amazing to have had the privilege. I also remember one friend getting a colour television; us kids would go over and sit in her lounge room looking in amazement at the new technology. We had extremely happy memories of living there.
From the 1960s, the coal mining industry was slowly deteriorating in England as the English produced coal could not compete on a global economic scale. The cheaper sources of energy at that time were the North Sea oil and gas. By the 1970s, there were ongoing mining strikes that crippled the economic welfare of the workers. Eventually, over time, mines started closing in England. This was during the Margaret Thatcher era. She was the English Prime Minister and was known for

her intolerance of the Unions, specifically from Dad's perspective, the National Mining Union.

Dad didn't see any future in the English coal mining industry and Australia was now looking for experienced coal miners. The advertisements offered mining families the opportunity to immigrate. He caught a bus into Leeds, where he was interviewed for a job at South Bulli Colliery, NSW, Australia. Dad was accepted quickly, and we were soon packing our bags for the journey ahead. Everyone was looking forward to the warm weather and beach lifestyle. This was going to be a big adventure for our young family.

Arnold and Joan on a country walk at St Margarets, Kent. [Photograph taken by 5 year old Alison].

Newmillerdam, Yorkshire, John, Alison, Paul and Arnold.

9
AUSTRALIA VERSUS ENGLAND

Emigration to Australia (1972)

Arnold 38, Joan 35, Paul 16, John 14, Alison 8

After selling our house and all the furniture, it was time to farewell our English family for an adventure to the other side of the world. On the 2nd of June 1972, we emigrated to Australia all feeling very excited. Only Dad had been on an aeroplane before during his time in the British Army, but travelling by air was a first for the rest of our family. 1972 was one of the worst years on record for plane crashes. There were 30 plane crashes, causing 2373 deaths. Thankfully, being only eight years old, I was not aware of that news.

We left England with only our suitcases full of our essential clothes. This must have been a massive, brave leap of faith for my parents to sell their house and all the contents for an unknown new beginning. They believed a better life was awaiting us all in Australia.

We boarded our first flight in London, travelling on a small plane to New York, then changing planes to a larger one for our next flight to Nadi, Fiji. Landing at Nadi airport, I remember feeling the warm, thick, humid air as we walked down off the plane across the tarmac into the air-conditioned airport. We had never felt humidity before; this was our first experience of tropical weather. Dad bought me a beautiful Fijian doll at the airport. We soon left Nadi heading to our destination of Sydney, Australia.

Arriving at Sydney airport, we collected our bags and went through Customs. We walked out into the main airport hall and to our surprise, we were met by the Manager of the South Bulli Coal Mine. The Manager was holding a sign with our family name on it. He was there to drive us to the Fairy Meadow Hostel, where they housed all the migrants arriving into the Illawarra region. The Manager said, "You are coming with me," and pointed to his beautiful, large, black car. It was a Mercedes. Other passengers from our flight had to queue at the bus stop, awaiting a coach ride to take them to the hostel.

Travelling by car was a rare treat for us. We felt Dad must have been a highly sought-after employee for the Coal Mine Manager to personally collect us at the airport. It was at least one to two hours of driving from Sydney to Fairy Meadow.

Paul, John and Mum sat in the back seat, so Dad sat in the front with the manager. The only place left for me was on Dad's lap. I was eight-years-old, holding tightly onto my new doll. I distinctly remember feeling a little too grownup to be sitting on his lap. We stopped at Bulli Tops escarpment so we could get out of the car to take in the panoramic view of the Illawarra region nestled alongside the Pacific Ocean, our new home.

The Fairy Meadow Hostel was filled with Nissen Huts. These semi-circle shaped huts were made of corrugated metal. When it rained, the sound on the metal was deafeningly loud, something we were not used to. Mum remembers the hut smelt musty when she first opened the door. It was a two-bedroom hut. Mum and Dad in one bedroom and Paul, John and I in the other. There were no cooking facilities or bathrooms in the hut. We had a communal dining room where meals were cooked for all the residents of the hostel and several shower-toilet blocks to share on site. It was like living in a caravan park.

The hostel was directly across the road from Fairy Meadow beach. We wondered why the beaches were empty on sunny days. It was an Australian winter, but to us it felt like an English summer. We were swimming and sunbathing on empty beaches with other European migrants from the Fairy Meadow Hostel.

Paul and John made some great friendships at the hostel. Still today, they have kept in touch with some of their friends from those early days and weeks on Fairy Meadow Hostel.

There was a mixed business "corner store", near the hostel we often walked to. It was here we found out that lollies were sweets. I thought I was getting an iced lolly (ice block) which was quite a treat. Much to my disappointment, I could only get sweets with my Australian coins.

I walked to and from Towradgi Primary School with the other kids from the hostel. It was at least 1.5 kilometres each way, being quite a long walk for an eight-year-old. The cooks at the hostel kitchen made my picnic lunch for school, which was usually a jam sandwich, piece of madeira cake and an orange. Friday was the best day of the week because I was given enough tuckshop money to buy a cream bun for morning tea and a meat pie for lunch. I loved Fridays for this one reason.

Paul and John were still within high school age. John went to Keira Boys High School in Wollongong (when he wasn't going to the beach). Mum and Dad caught John on the beach many times when he should have been at school.

Mum and Dad wanted Paul to continue studying at high school. He refused and could not be coerced into further study, so he found himself a full-time job in a bank. They were extremely proud of him getting that job. This meant he would be a white-collar worker (middle social class); having to wear a jacket, tie and collared shirt to work. It was a first for our family. A labouring job, like coal mining, was a blue-collar worker (working social class).

Mum and Dad soon became tired of our restricted hostel lifestyle. The communal eating and designated washrooms lost their appeal very quickly. It was fun for the kids, though, having lots of people to hang out with. After six weeks in the hostel, Dad found us a new home.

We moved into a two-bedroom flat in Montague Street, next to Fairy Meadow train station, just around the corner from the hostel. Strangely, it hadn't occurred to my parents that it might have been possible to find a three-bedroom flat. I shared a bedroom with Paul and John, with a dividing wardrobe for my privacy. Mum put pink floral wallpaper on the back of the wardrobe for me.

One Sunday morning, Dad put on his best English brown suit to walk to the local pub for a pre-lunch beer (as you do in England). Mum was cooking a beautiful Sunday roast. As he walked into the pub, everyone stopped talking and turned to face him as if he was going to make an announcement. He felt so embarrassed, walked up to the bar, and ordered a beer. Dad only stayed for one drink and left promptly. Dress codes were another cultural shock which we had to modify to suit the Australian lifestyle.

In England, Mum had worked in nursing homes as an assistant nurse ever since I started school. Once we had settled into the new flat in Fairy Meadow, she started looking for a nursing home job. She visited local shops asking for nursing home locations nearby and was directed to Chesalon Nursing Home that was in Woonona.

She walked a very long way to find Chesalon. I'm presuming she caught a bus to Woonona shops on the Princes Highway from Fairy Meadow, then walked east to the nursing home, possibly two to three kilometres. Walking those distances nowadays is unthinkable. Arriving at the nursing home, she met the matron who proudly showed her around the home, introducing her as Mrs Hinchcliffe to the staff as their new staff member. To Mum's surprise, she was hired on the spot.

Dad was chuffed that Mum had a job because it really helped them to save for their own house again. I remember feeling so rich when my parents were able to buy a bucket of apples or oranges from the

Fairy Meadow Fruit Market and a large tub of ice cream in our weekly groceries. Living in England, Mum didn't buy a lot of fruit. It may have been more expensive. She said we were lucky to have one piece of fruit per week.

Mum loved her new job and made wonderful long-lasting friendships at Chesalon particularly; Maureen, Betty and Beth. They were her best-buddies, remembered forever in her heart to this day. Sadly, they have all since passed, many years ago.

In the 1970s, women wore long maxi party dresses for day or evening events. Mum and her friends from Chesalon would put on their finery and fashionable maxi dresses to go to their luncheon parties, taking turns to host these regular events. At these parties, Mum would take her movie camera to capture their joyful antics over a nice meal and a few drinks. A couple of years ago, I was able to get these 8mm and 16mm films put onto DVD for Mum to rewatch the memories she had recorded. Those old films were in colour but without sound.

Dad was 38-years-old and just learning to drive a car for the first time. The long distances to work on shift work and lack of public transport meant having a car was an essential need for daily life. The first car Dad bought was quite old. You could see the road through the rusted holes in the flooring. Dad drove embarrassingly slowly as he learnt to drive. John remembers a very slow drive from Wollongong to Nowra Caravan Park on our first holiday in Australia. After Dad got his license, Mum learnt to drive too, but upgraded our car to one without rust or holes in the floor.

Dad soon found us a spacious three-bedroom house to rent in Elizabeth Street, Towradgi, with a large garden. He was keen to have a garden and put us kids in our own bedrooms. We got a dog at this house called Scruffy. I'm not sure where he came from or where he went, as he didn't come with us to our next house. Maybe he was a stray dog that just wandered in. He had black, fuzzy, curly hair with a little patch of brown around his face. Dad was happy to have his own garden and soon planted a few flower beds. He painted my bedroom a lovely deep lavender colour.

Living on the other side of Towradgi, I changed schools for the new catchment area, and went to Fairy Meadow Demonstration School. To me, it felt like a very large school with huge grounds and new modern buildings. It was a long walk, maybe 1.1 kilometres each way. Mum and Dad gave me bus fares, but in the summer months, I often chose to walk home so I could buy a paddle pop ice cream at the corner store near our house.

By now, John had started a butcher's apprenticeship at Paul's Butcher Shop Fairy Meadow, across the road from my school. Paul (the butcher shop owner) was a tall Italian man thickly set, with a strong Italian accent. I felt scared of his loud deep voice and would hide behind Mum or Dad, trying to avoid eye contact. The local migrant community of Fairy Meadow enjoyed buying their weekly meat and delicatessen supplies from his shop. He seemed to be a good boss. He often cooked a steak and eggs for breakfast for himself and John, when John arrived early enough in the mornings for work.

On the weekends, I used to play in the backyard, making cubby houses out of old sheets tying them to the trees and bushes. It wasn't long before Dad built me a wooden framed cubby house. The walls were made from tarp like material nailed to the frame. It was much better than sheets draped over the trees.

Our second Christmas in Australia was in this house. Unfortunately, this was the year I was becoming unsure about the reality of Santa Claus (Father Christmas). A few classmates at school informed me Santa was make believe and that my parents bought and wrapped all the presents for their children.

After school one day, I demanded the truth from my mum as I really didn't know what to believe, feeling extremely concerned. She was quite tired, lying on the lounge after having just finished a shift at the nursing home. I asked for the truth, and I got it. I was absolutely devastated at nine-years-old finding out Santa was our parents. Little did Mum know that I would have kept believing if Mum had told me the kids at school had got it wrong. I soon got over the shock of Santa not existing on Christmas morning when I saw a beautiful orange bicycle and lots of other presents under the Christmas tree.

During our time in this house, we experienced an earthquake. The noise woke me up. It felt like someone was banging violently on my bedroom walls from the outside. I dived out of my bed and ran as fast as I could to my parent's bedroom, jumping into their bed with absolute terror. After the rattling walls had stopped, there was an eerie long silence. The neighbours went out onto the streets trying to find out the reason for the loud noises. Some believed it was an accident or an explosion in the local coal mine. Just the thought of something awful going wrong at the mine was very distressing to us all, being a mining family. Thankfully, it was not a mining accident. It was a 5.5 magnitude earthquake that hit west of Picton, NSW, 50 kilometres away.

By 1974, Dad came home one day and announced to Mum that we now owned a house in Bulli. The address was 44 Willcath Street. Strangely, Mum hadn't even looked at the house. It was a surprise for us all. We were so excited to have our own house, no more renting. This meant it would be much closer for Mum and Dad to get to their workplaces. It was a three-bedroom house, elevated on a hill with ocean views (from my bedroom windows). There was a very large backyard that sloped down towards a creek. The bridge over the creek was close to our house, that I would walk across on my way to school, Woniora Public School, being a 10-minute walk from home. We often walked to the beach and the rock swimming pools at Bulli Beach. We all loved living near the beach.

The new house meant we needed a dog by Dad's standards. Mum and Dad loved Cocker Spaniels, so Dad bought a red roan Cocker Spaniel puppy, which we named Jason. I can't imagine Dad not having a dog by his side, he certainly loved his dogs.

I modestly trained Jason and took him to Bulli Dog Show one year. All the dogs had to stand to attention in a line with their head and tail up, striking a pose. They all faced the one direction, to the right, however Jason turned around facing the opposite direction, to the left. The judge soon told me that he was facing the wrong way, but I found it too hard to turn him around, so I embarrassingly let him stand facing the dog behind him nose to nose. We didn't get any prize ribbons, but it was fun participating with all the other dogs.

Both Paul and John had motorbikes, enjoying the life and freedom of being teenagers and young adults. One day, Mum gave John some money with an order of meat to bring home from his butcher shop. He put the meat order in his backpack and jumped on his motorbike to ride home. Unfortunately, he forgot to zip up his backpack. By the time he got home, all the meat had fallen out. The trail of meat would have been a lovely surprise to any dogs that found the meat on the road.

Paul was riding his motorbike up Macquarie Pass, a very steep road with hairpin bends. When he hit a sunken drain, he went flying over the motorbike's handlebars. Luckily, he got away with only a broken collarbone and a lot of road gravel embedded into his back, arms, and legs.

I was a mad horse lover, along with my good friend Kim. In Bulli, empty large blocks of land (paddocks) surrounded us, so many locals could keep their horses nearby. We would visit all the local horses, secretly feeding them bread or carrots without the horse owners' knowledge. We weren't scared of climbing through the fences and walking straight up to the horses. Eventually, we knew all their names.

One day, we had the wonderful experience of watching a mare deliver her foal. We hid behind large bushes in her paddock as she gave birth. It was hard trying to be quiet, as we didn't want to disturb or distract the mare, but we couldn't take our eyes off her, watching with intense intrigue. The membrane bag that delivered the foal confused me, wondering how the foal would breathe, but she soon kicked her way out of it. We were thrilled to see the foal. The horse's owner knew we were hiding but was happy enough for us to stay there watching from a good distance. We were able to come up to the foal the next day and get much closer.

Dad loved his horses too, so I guess this is where I get that passion from. I was so wanting my own horse, but Mum and Dad refused my constant requests. Mum offered to buy me a piano, suggesting I could learn to play and have lessons. Mmm... horse or piano—there's quite a difference.

After settling into our new house at Bulli Beach, it was time for a holiday back to England to catch up with family and enjoy the English countryside of familiar places. I was so lucky, as Dad was only too pleased for me to have beautiful clothes, especially when on holiday in England. I had a new long corduroy blue coat with green and blue tartan patterns on the lapels matched up with my new high-heeled winter boots. I felt very grown up, like a teenager, at age 11.

Being a horse lover, Mum and Dad bought me a Barbie doll with her Barbie horse. I absolutely loved it. I was always on the lookout for more horse ornaments to add to my collection when we visited the English antique and china shops. This holiday made both Mum and Dad feel very homesick for our English family and culture.

Paul left home in December 1976 to start a 12-month contract with the Commonwealth Bank in Kimbe and Port Moresby, Papua New Guinea. Paul celebrated his 21st birthday in Papua New Guinea with his new banking family, Peter and Lynn. They were an aunt and uncle of his future wife that he hadn't met yet. When Paul arrived back in Sydney 12 months later, he made his move to ask out their niece, Deborah, for a luncheon date. The rest is history, marriage, two children and seven grandchildren later.

Ping Pong Pom (1977)

Dad sold our beautiful beach house at Bulli. The emotional pull to the English family and English culture was too great. I had just finished primary school and was due to enrol into high school. I would have started Bulli High School at the end of January 1977, going into 1st Form (Grade 7). Instead, our family moved back to England for a new beginning. Mum, John and I travelled back first, then Dad followed a little later. Paul was still in Papua New Guinea completing his 12 month bank posting.

As soon as Dad arrived in England, he drove out to his old Pit, Betteshanger, looking for another start, knowing it had been eight years since he had worked there before. Dad was employed on the spot as an Overman (supervisor). They were pleased and excited to have him back. He just picked up where he left off, knowing most of the men who still worked there. Now Dad had a few of his own tales to tell the men from his coal mining experiences working in Australia.

While our family was looking for a house to buy, we stayed with my grandparents at the Ropewalk in Dover. I loved being at my grandparents' house. They were so kind to me. I really enjoyed Grandma's cooking, especially her Christmas fruit cake. Grandad played chess with me. I had been taught a few good moves from my primary school teacher in Australia, so Grandad encouraged my chess playing strategies.

Mum and Dad searched for quite some time, looking at many possibilities to buy a house in Dover. They finally decided on a semi-detached terrace in Farthingloe Road, Maxton, just on the outskirts of Dover. It had a long narrow backyard that Dad was keen to fill with flowers.

We had only travelled back to England with our suitcases, no furniture or household items. So, everything had to be bought new. It was exciting choosing new furniture, linen, cutlery, crockery, ornaments, washing machine, stove, TV and everything you can imagine. Dad was very proud of his hardworking life as a coal miner, being able to buy so many beautiful new things to fill our English house. Mum and Dad loved their new home. They were ready to finally settle down in England permanently, patiently awaiting the arrival of Paul, after his 12-month bank posting was complete.

Mum was thrilled to see her sisters and parents again. John found a job as a butcher in a supermarket, but then moved on to a metal fabrication workshop for better wages. I was 13-years-old when I started high school.

We all had lots of fun going abroad, across the English Channel, for day trips to France and Belgium from the port of Dover. Mum and

Dad slipped back into the English lifestyle quickly. John and I were very happy when we started to make our new friends and we both loved the stylish English clothes and shops.

My new school was Castlemount Secondary School. Mum went to this newly built school in 1948, being one of the first students to arrive wearing the very smart new red and grey uniform. She left school in 1951. Both Paul and John went to this school in the 1960s, Paul then went on to Dover Boys Grammar. It was finally my turn in the 1970s to attend Castlemount to maintain our family tradition.

Dressed in my lovely English long red coat, smart grey skirt, low heeled black shoes and white blouse, I headed to Castlemount Secondary School for my first day in high school. I skipped 1st Form and went into 2nd Form because of my age. As I waited to go into my first class, queuing up with the other children, the teacher invited me in and announced to the class that I was a new student from Australia. After talking to the classmates later in the playground, they had thought I was a student teacher, being so dressed up. I soon learned that the children didn't dress up for school.

However, when it came to jewellery and makeup, they were very strict. They disallowed nail polish or earrings, not even basic sleepers or studs for the girls. We used to let our long hair out loosely covering our ears, hoping no teacher would see our sleepers from newly pierced ears. There were only one or two teachers that would check or make a fuss. I was asked once by a male teacher to take out my sleepers. Sadly, I complied, but was extremely annoyed at this silly rule.

All those years later, I even had the same teacher as my mum. He was the geography teacher for me. Mum told me he was a very good-looking young teacher in her time, that all the girls used to love. Thirty years later, he seemed like a very old man to me, ready for retirement.

During the winter season, our school was doing some cross-country training. It had been snowing and covered the ground with about 10 centimetres of snow. It felt very cold to me, being an Aussie chick.

To my horror, we weren't allowed to wear anything but our red PE shorts, white PE t-shirts and joggers for the cross-country long run around the town of Dover. The orders were—no jumpers, hats, or gloves. I felt this fierce discipline by the PE teachers was cruel. Long distance running was never my favourite sport, especially in the snow. To top off this particularly difficult day, when I got to the top of Castle hill, I was told I needed to go back down to the school to get my school photograph taken in the hall. I raced down the hill into the school hall, had a photograph snapped, then had to race back up the hill to try and catch up with the runners. I was both late and scared of getting lost on the run; however, I did finish the race somehow.

I loved gymnastics and dance classes in the school hall or netball and rounders on the huge grass fields. Generally, the sport department was fun. I also enjoyed all the sciences. I didn't realise until leaving this school that I had done well in the science exams, coming second in physics and third in chemistry.

Dad's brother, Douglas, with his family, had moved to South Africa from England to manage a coal mine. They later moved to Australia in the mid-1970s. Dad had persuaded Douglas to join the Australian mining industry near where we lived. They were settled in Bulli, Australia, when we moved back to England in 1977.

The rest of Dad's immediate family, including his parents, lived in Yorkshire, England. Dover to Yorkshire in the 1970s was a good day's drive or a long day's train trip from London. His parents, Olga and Stanley, came to visit us for a two-week holiday in our new home in Dover. It was lovely to have them around. They really enjoyed their holiday with us and spending time in Deal, where they used to live with fond memories after World War II.

Mum and Dad loved going for long country walks. We could walk up over the hill at the back of Maxton, down into the Ropewalk on the other side of Dover. Sometimes we collected blackberries that were growing wild along the ridge on top of the hill. A blackberry and apple pie were a family favourite that Mum often cooked for us, served with cream or custard.

As I write my dad's story, I can understand why he had such a deep heritage—loving all things English. Having been a Grenadier Guard for the Queen in his early years, his loyalty to England was embedded in his psyche.

We were all so excited to see Paul when he had completed his 12-month work contract in Papua New Guinea. Everyone expected Paul to move in with his family, wherever that may be. Paul had no intention of staying in England. His home was Australia and had a good job lined up to start in the following February 1978, as an Audit Assistant in Sydney. Paul was now an independent young adult living his own life, freedom from parents at 21. We were all very shocked that he wasn't staying in England with his family.

Soon after Paul had returned to Australia, Mum decided she couldn't let him live in Australia without his family. Once those thoughts crystalised, our house was put on the market for sale. It sold within two weeks. I was completely devastated, as I had made some close friends and was loving my new teenage life in England. The thought of changing schools again and finding new friends was difficult for me to comprehend at 14. John was happy enough to move back to Australia. He was always happy to go with the family flow, being content with any decision. Dad was probably very reluctant to leave his homeland once again, especially having just set up such a beautiful home full of new things, but he knew "happy wife—happy life" was the easier path forward.

Double Back (1978)

Dad 44, Mum 41, Paul 22, John 20, Alison 14

Paul collected us from Sydney airport in his orange Ford Cortina. I remember feeling very grown up, wearing stiletto sandals, a flared cream mid-length skirt, aqua blouse and a pink fluffy jacket. Paul thought I'd grown up a lot since he had seen me several months prior; that put a proud smile on my face instantly. He drove us to a two-bedroom flat overlooking Towradgi Beach on Marine Parade. Being a cloudy, windy winter's day, the surf was wildly crashing onto the beach. It was just the four of us now; Dad, Mum, John and I. Paul was independently renting his own small flat near his work in Sydney. It was another new start. The flat was quite small for the four of us, so Dad searched for a house with a garden to rent.

He found a three-bedroom bungalow in Raymond Parade, Towradgi, with a good-sized garden. It gave John and me our privacy, having a bedroom each, which we certainly needed at our ages.

Dad suggested that John join him in the coal mining industry for a new career. John and Dad both got jobs easily at the Helensburgh Colliery. Like father, like son, John was now a coal miner. A new beginning for John. He soon learnt how to drive all the machinery down the Pit. John prided himself on being able to carry a 70-kilogram roof bolt on his shoulder for 200 metres.

Thanks to John working alongside Dad, both the miners and the office staff nicknamed my father, "Dad". He loved working with his son. John had the utmost respect from all the workers, as he always worked hard. John was young and fit with a kind, friendly nature. Dad was extremely proud of his son's personality and work ethics. Now working together, they developed a very beautiful close relationship, much like Dad had when he worked with his father in England.

Dad made a particularly good friend at Helensburgh coal mine, Nifty-Nev, who was a little older than Dad. Neville was a Loco driver (a loco is a low, heavy haulage engine used in underground mining) and Dad was often his assistant. They used to lay rails and deliver equipment around the mine. At Helensburgh pub, there was a special corner in the pub where the coal miners would drink after work. Engraved on the window are the names of the coal miners who served long careers at the local coal mine. Neville was one of them.

Mum got her old job back at Chesalon Nursing Home in Woonona. It was a new school for me; Corrimal High School, going into 3rd Form (Grade 9). It was at this school where I met my first husband, Mark, and made some special long-term friendships.

Due to changing countries and schools, I ended up completely missing my first year of high school, doing six months of 2nd Form (Grade 8) and 18 months of 3rd Form. It seems I lost six months of schooling somewhere between England and Australia, thanks to the differing school terms. I left school at the end of 4th Form (Grade 10) when I was 15-years-old.

Dad invited Mum's parents, Alf and Mary, to Australia for a holiday to join in our family celebrations. John married Evelyne, in April 1980, in Wollongong and three weeks later Paul married Deborah, in May 1980, in Sydney. After the two weddings, Mum and Dad flew back to England with Grandma and Grandad for a holiday.

With Paul and John both married and moving into their own flats, it was just Dad, Mum and me now, so Dad bought a two-bedroom red-brick flat in a small block of four, near Bellambi Beach in Gladstone Street.

After leaving high school in 1979, I agreed to study a secretarial diploma at Williams Business College in Wollongong in 1980, with Dad's encouragement. It was a 12-month full-time course. Every weeknight, my homework was spread over the dining table. Mum enjoyed me being home with her in the evenings because Dad worked afternoon shifts. This one year of study was very strict, giving me a solid foundation for the many years ahead when I worked in administrative roles. I was very grateful that Dad gave me the opportunity to go to this expensive private college that had a good reputation with high standards. I often say Dad paid for this or that, not Mum, only because he was the money manager in our home. Both Mum and Dad always worked full-time ever since I started school.

Mum and Dad celebrated their 25 years of marriage, a silver wedding anniversary, at a Chinese restaurant in Corrimal. They received silver gifts from Paul, John and me; a tray, teapot, sugar bowl and milk jug. Dad bought Mum an eternity ring; a lovely gold band with three ruby stones and two diamonds that she wears next to her gold wedding ring. She had lost her original engagement ring a long time ago. Now her fingers are painfully swollen at the joints with rheumatism, but she still wears her eternity ring and wedding band ring together. Mum remembers Dad buying her the eternity ring when they were on holiday in Yorkshire, England earlier that year in 1980.

Dad's parents sadly passed away in 1981. He travelled back to England for the funerals by himself. His father, Stanley, passed away on the 7th of January 1981 and his mother, Olga, nine months later, on the 16th of September 1981. It was during this time I started having disturbing dreams that told me of pending family deaths. I was 17-years-old.

Dad's mum was a medium in her later years (from 40 years onwards) and was often invited to be a guest medium at local Spiritual Churches in England. She was able to communicate with those that had passed over, giving helpful messages to individual members of the congregation, allowing healing and reassurance that death was not final but only a transition to another plane of existence. Dad was very intuitive and loved to tell me "he knew" things were going to happen. His mother may have taught him on a subtle level to listen to his innate intuition and to trust his gut instincts. There is some psychic awareness in our family tree that has been passed down through the generations from my grandmother's line.

After his parents passed on, it wasn't long before Dad's grandchildren started arriving from Paul and John. This is when I started to notice patterns of death and birth to honour family equilibrium. The first grandchild was Dione, born to John and Evelyne in October 1981. The second grandchild was Peter, born to Paul and Deborah a year later, in October 1982. The third grandchild was Claire, born to John and Evelyne in November 1983.

My plan was to leave home at 17, but Mum didn't think that was a good idea until I was married. So, I became engaged soon after, then married my boyfriend, Mark, on the 10th of September 1983. My wedding was one week after Mum and Dad's 28th wedding anniversary. My parents were now empty nesters.

During the winter of 1984, I moved to Mudgee, central west New South Wales (NSW), with Mark for his job at Ulan coal mine, as a qualified electrician. Mark's brother was a Deputy in the mine and helped pull a few strings to get him a start at the Pit. I left my wonderful job and short career of three and half years, working as a senior legal secretary. My employers at the time wanted me to study law, but it was not meant to be.

Paul and Deborah were living in Minto, near Campbeltown, and soon moved to West Wyalong for Paul's first bank manager's posting. Paul was a bank manager at 30, which was very rare in the 1980s. John and Evelyne remained in the Illawarra area, in Corrimal, with their young girls, and John still worked with Dad at the Pit in Helensburgh.

Dad's very long career as a coal miner was catching up to him. He was now 50. Coalface underground mining is a laboriously intensive job. Dad was not one for slowing down or taking it easy at work. He was there to work hard, doing his utmost best. The men were paid bonuses if they could get a high volume of coal out in their shift. This was the driving factor to work hard, always. I remember Dad was very proud when they had achieved bonuses (more money) for their hard-working shift.

Unfortunately, he was now experiencing constant back pain, not just at work, but at home too. John was Dad's firsthand witness to the treatment the mine management dished out to him when he started requesting lighter duties at the Pit to give him a chance to recover from his severe back pain.

Sadly, the Pit's management didn't provide adequate light duties because they didn't believe his pain was real. Having studied pain management at university myself, the key take-home message was "pain is whatever the patient says it is, whether or not there is a physical reason, and that if the acute pain is not resolved quickly enough, it will definitely end with chronic pain that is much harder to heal."

Ultimately, this is what brought his mining career to an end at 50 to 51 years of age. He was left with no alternative but to put in a workers' compensation claim to enable an early retirement. In those days, putting in a workers' compensation claim was a very low act, as if the claim was a personal attack on the managers themselves. Management, alongside their insurance and legal teams, would fight to the bitter end, making life as difficult as possible for any employee who put in a claim.

They sent private investigators out to secretly film Dad if he was mowing his lawn or digging in his garden, for example. The manager gave Dad a very difficult time, testing him with not so light duty jobs working on the Pit top, to trick him into failing the workers' compensation claim.

My parents now had to plan for an enforced early retirement, so they sold their Bellambi flat. They were going to build a new house in the country seaside town of Shoalhaven Heads, further down the south coast of the NSW. They decided to rent a small flat in McKinnon Street, Woonona, a short walk to the main shopping centre of Woonona, while they awaited the finalisation of the compensation claim.

When feeling low, planning a holiday back to England always brightened Dad up. Off-season, cheap airfares to England was a winter trip, in January to February, so Mum and Dad decided to go to England for Grandma Pearson's 71st birthday, in January 1985. Her party was at The Ropewalk with all of Mum's sisters. In January, the snow had fallen and settled in for a cold winter's holiday. That didn't stop Mum and Dad enjoying another lovely holiday in England, giving Dad a break from work for a few weeks.

Later the same year, it was my grandparents' Alfred and Mary Pearson's 50th Wedding Anniversary, in December. To join the English family celebrations, Mum, Dad, John, Evelyne, Dione, Claire, Mark and I travelled back to England for the party in Dover. We all stayed on for Christmas that year. Mum's sisters and families were there, and it was wonderful to see everyone. It was Evelyne and Mark's first holiday to England, an opportunity to meet their English relatives. We had an absolute ball. John and Evelyne had also travelled to France and Italy to see Evelyne's families. Mark and I did a couple of trips to France, Belgium, Holland and Switzerland, making the most of being on that side of the planet.

This is an excerpt from Mum's diary, "7th December 1985—Holiday to England. Sydney airport, stopover in Abu Dhabi. Dad bought a bottle of whisky and a bottle of Tia Maria duty free. I bought a bottle of scent for $18. Arrived back home in Australia on 10th January 1986."

Arnold's new car, HR Holden, in Australia.

Arnold with his parents; Stanley and Olga in Yorkshire, England.

"Ee Bah Gum" The Yorkshireman

Joan and Arnold, on a Cross Channel Ferry day-trip, Kent, England.

Helensburgh Pit, John (left), Arnold (eighth from left), Australia

Alison Simpson

10
ENFORCED EARLY RETIREMENT

Dad 52, Mum 50, Paul 30, John 29, Alison 22

While Dad was still negotiating with the coal mine to perform light duties, to no avail, Mum and Dad decided to move closer to the beach. They rented a small house near Woonona Beach in Campbell Street. The house sat on top of a hill with magical ocean views and plenty of fresh sea breezes. Mum enjoyed volunteering at her old workplace nearby, Chesalon Nursing Home. She helped make the morning beds for a few days every week.

This house was on a very large block of land with an enormous area of grass to be mowed. Mum was fit, and happy to mow the lawns for Dad. He soon got to work planting his flowers, vegetables, and herbs in a large garden bed. My parents often harvested their vegetables for dinner. Dad loved his gardens, a passion that has been passed down through the generations.

Dad's love of swimming continued. He swam laps at the Rock Pools of Bulli or Woonona, because this was much easier for him than swimming through the crashing waves in the open beaches.

Daily walking became an essential part of their lifestyle. As I look back at the distances that they walked daily, it was amazing. Today, walking to shops or the beach is hardly considered achievable or even normal; we just jump in a car to go anywhere. I mapped their distances from Mum's diary as she noted their daily activities.

Woonona Circle, a small shopping centre, was 1.5 kilometres away, and it took them about 15-minutes to walk. Woonona Rock Pool, a 10 to 15-minute walk, about 1.1 kilometres. Bulli Rock Pool, a little further away, 15 to 20-minute walk, about 1.4 kilometres. Woonona Bulli RSL Club, a 1.1 kilometre walk, that was about 15 minutes walking distance. If you included the return walks, they were doing at least 30 minutes of daily walking, sometimes double that if they walked to the beach and then the club for lunch in the afternoons. They both loved being outdoors in the sun and fresh air.

Mum and Dad enjoyed watching movies in the afternoon or evenings, especially after a physical morning of walking, swimming, or gardening. Mum would stay up late at night watching movies where Dad would go to bed earlier.

Dad referred to the habitual afternoon nap after lunch as "40 winks". The official time of 40 winks is about 16 seconds, but his afternoon naps were much longer than that, 30 to 60 minutes. It was a Hinchcliffe thing because I remember his parents would always have 40 winks too. Today I call it a power nap to recharge before I attempt my next round of work or activity for the afternoon.

On one family Sunday roast lunch at Mum and Dad's house, I remember us all sitting at the dining table (my brothers, sisters-in-law, nieces, nephew, husband and I) when Dad burst into tears with his pain. This was the first time I had ever seen my dad cry in such agony. It was heartbreaking for us all to witness. We all looked at each in absolute horror at the sound of our father in unbearable pain and crying.

Spinal Surgery

Dad cancelled his earlier appointment for spinal surgery, hoping he could recover somehow without the need of intervention. Unfortunately, this didn't work. His back pain didn't improve, so he felt forced into a corner with no other options but to take the risk that spinal surgery would fix his agonising pain.

Dad could not endure any more pain caused from the wear and tear of decades of coal mining, and the physical overload from poor mining conditions. On the 25th of March Mum and Dad caught a train to Sydney, then a bus to Rose Bay Private Hospital to check in the day before surgery. Mum left him at hospital but returned the next day. This time catching three trains and one bus to get to the hospital. During Dad's surgery he had two vertebrae discs fused together with pins securing them, possibly L3 and L4. Having two discs fused together significantly reduced his flexion and range of movement in his back.

After surgery Mum remembers how sad he looked, perhaps still groggy from the surgery. The following day, Mum had a rest day at home and organised to stay with Paul and Deborah for the remaining days while Dad was in hospital. Dad was in hospital for a total of four nights.

Mum drove up to Minto, near Campbeltown (western Sydney) staying for two nights. From here she was able to get a lift with Paul and Deborah to hospital during visiting hours. Mum loved staying with Paul and Deborah, especially being able to play with her grandson, Peter. It was a lovely break for her having their support at this difficult time.

On the 1st of April, Dad was allowed home. Thankfully, John drove Mum up to the hospital from Wollongong to collect him, as he couldn't walk, catch a train or bus. It was a difficult car ride home. He was supported in the car with lots of pillows, but he still cried in pain with any bump or car turn. This was incredibly distressing for both Mum and John. I am wondering if he really had enough pain relief from the hospital. Nowadays, I would expect strong pain relief to remove any discomfort.

From the mid-1980s, Mum started writing her daily reflections in her diaries. Mum loved writing her daily activities in her diaries, but they were used against Dad's compensation claim from Paul's memory. Apparently, her dates were not always correct. The Mining Tribunal who examined Dad's claim used this as a factor to disallow a good lump sum payment. He was given a small payout, which he was reluctantly forced to accept. This was an extremely stressful time for Dad; physically, emotionally, and now financially. His proud mining career had ended on a disappointing, low note.

Mum and Dad often met up with Paul, Deborah, Peter, John, Evelyne, Dione and Claire at local dams in the National Parks for a Sunday picnic. I was living in Mudgee, a little too far to join them for only one day unless visiting for a weekend.

Everyone would load the picnic baskets and esky coolers into their cars for a lovely day out in nature, usually near a waterhole. In the 1980s, all shops and businesses closed on Saturday afternoon and didn't reopen again until Monday. Sunday was the perfect day to spend time relaxing with family. I remember there was a competition to see who had the best smelling barbeque, nicest picnic table setting, or most fun with games of cricket or football.

It took Dad two months post-surgery before he felt he could manage a long road trip to Mudgee, about three to four hours of driving, to visit me. He was unable to drive, so Mum drove all the way, having many stops, so they could both get out of the car to stretch. They stopped at the Majestic Restaurant Cafe Lookout high in the Blue Mountains overlooking the beautiful national parks, then a quick stop at Hartley to buy some apples. Dad loved his daily apple, always reminding me "an apple a day keeps the doctor away". This term was coined in 1866, and my dad was still using it 120 years later.

The last stop was usually the town of Lithgow for the final leg into Mudgee. I always enjoyed having Mum and Dad visit us on our farm just outside of Mudgee. We had dogs, cats, horses, chickens and sheep. Dad loved the animals and was always keen to give me advice. When he came on my animal walks, with the dogs, cats and sometimes my horse, down the dusty dirt roads, my kelpie would always walk behind the human pack leader. It was Dad, every time. The kelpie trotted right next to him off lead, not leaving his side. My springer spaniel often ran off being very naughty, having selective hearing when it suited her. Mudgee is a wine district, so we often visited the local vineyards for some wine tasting and picked up a couple of bottles of wine to enjoy whilst they were on holidays with us.

For a treat, Dad took Mum out for morning tea in Wollongong to a posh cafe, International Coffee House. They had coffee and a beautiful strawberry topped cake. Mum said it was lovely, costing them $10, which was quite a lot in those days. Dad was celebrating a small workers' compensation cheque for his thumb injury, having lost a large piece off his thumb. He got $10,000, which was something worth celebrating.

Mum and Dad often dropped into one of their favourite clubs to have a drink and play on the poker machines. Mum loved playing the poker machines and still does. Sometimes, she gambled a few dollars, but Dad usually only put in a few coins. He was often the lucky one to win, but Mum certainly had a few wins too.

On the 3rd of September 1986, it was Mum and Dad's wedding anniversary. Dad bought Mum a beautiful card. Mum reminds me that she forgot to buy a card that year because she was only three days away from hosting a wedding party for Douglas and his second wife, Veronica, at their house. Her own wedding anniversary had not crossed her mind.

Dad was a very romantic and considerate husband. I could see how much he loved her. Sometimes he would buy her flowers, treat her to some new clothes, go out for lunch, or on a holiday.

Mum and Dad hosted Douglas and Veronica's wedding in their house and garden. Douglas wore a Filipino Shirt and Veronica wore a beautiful white gown. The wedding ceremony started at 3pm followed by a lovely meal, drinks and celebrations, ending at 9:30pm. Both Evelyne and Marilou, Veronica's friend, helped Mum with serving the meal and cleaning up the dishes at the end of the night. There were 30 guests, so it was a busy time of hosting for Mum and Dad.

Being very generous, Dad invited my grandparents, Alf and Mary, to come for an incredibly long three-month holiday from England, of which they accepted happily. Upon arrival at Sydney airport in March 1987, they were met by most of the family.

My grandparents were treated like royalty being whisked away on road trips to many lovely places. They travelled through the central west towns to visit Paul in West Wyalong and my farm in Mudgee. Travelling along dirt roads from Mudgee, they explored Hill End, an old gold mining town and the ten-dollar town, Gulgong (the town appeared on the first Australian $10 note).

Grandad Pearson wrote a diary of his day-to-day holiday activities, then handed the small blue diary back to Mum for a keepsake, before they flew back home to England. To this day, Mum still has his diary, and it's lovely to see his extremely neat handwriting. His journaling was diplomatic, with only kind words. The diary noted all the lovely meals they experienced and appreciated the wonderful driving adventures.

Now I understand where my enjoyment of writing comes from, the Pearson family line. Mum's sisters and their children are very talented creatives too; we have writers, artists, poets, painters, designers and decorators. It's a blessing to see the family lineage of talents.

I would have to say the most outstanding talent from the Hinchcliffe lineage is cooking. I fondly remember my Grandma Hinchcliffe's meals, along with Dad's siblings. They all cooked very Yorkshire style food that was just delicious. Paul and John love their cooking too. Emma, Paul's daughter, became a chef, taking the Hinchcliffe passion into a profession. I'm glad I taught my sons to cook from scratch, a helpful life skill for today's world.

Paul introduced Mum to golf, and she loved it, often playing a game with her neighbour, June, who lived across the road in Woonona. One weekend when Paul and family were visiting from West Wyalong, Mum had a game of golf with Paul and John. Dad stayed home with Evelyne, Deborah and the children getting a lunch of fish, chips and peas ready for everyone.

Dad finally bought himself a bicycle, so he could ride with Mum. It cost $250, being a five speed trail bike with thick tyres. John and Evelyne called around to see his new bike. There is a cycle track that follows the beach coastline from Bulli to Wollongong. They would cycle to Wollongong, then swim a few laps in the Continental Baths Rock Pool. After swimming, they would go for a cup of tea in a local cafe before riding home.

Cycling that distance would take a good 30 to 40 minutes each way. That is an amazing amount of exercise. No wonder they wanted 40 winks after lunch. Thanks to Mum and Dad, Paul, John and I are certainly chips off the old blocks, being keen to enjoy the great outdoor sports our parents did. Hopefully, the grandchildren and great-grandchildren will do the same, enjoying the outdoor Australian active lifestyles.

Brass and silver ornaments were a fashionable decor item in the 1980s home. To keep a visual high standard of shine, they needed cleaning regularly. This was often Dad's job. The result of freshly polished brass and silver always put a proud, content smile on Dad's face as he showed off his work. Perhaps this rekindled memories of his time in the Grenadier Guards, where he had to polish the brass buttons on his red tunic.

For the Australian Bicentennial celebrations, an Australian State Coach was designed and built in Dubbo, Australia, by W J Frecklington, as a gift to the Queen. The coach went on an Australian tour before being shipped over to England on a jumbo jet. Figtree, near Wollongong, was one of the tour destinations. Mum and Dad could not let this special event go by and went to see it for themselves. The coach was first used at the State Opening of the United Kingdom Parliament on the 8th of May 1988.

Dad loved visiting Paul and his family in Dubbo, especially on weekends, to watch Peter play football. Paul had moved there from West Wyalong, becoming the new bank manager in Dubbo, a much bigger region to manage. Dad was very proud of Paul's executive achievements in the bank.

Mum and Dad would then visit me on my 25-acre farm in Mudgee. The funny thing is both Deborah and I would often cook lasagna, an easy meal prepared earlier, for their first night at our homes. Lucky Mum and Dad liked lasagna. It became a regular pattern.

Dad loved all the animals on our farm, especially the horses and dogs. He had a permanent grin when he was on my farm, loving my hobby farm lifestyle. We considered building a granny house on our property for Mum and Dad, but unfortunately, that idea never became a reality. I was also considering growing grapes for a local vineyard, having studied at Orange Agriculture College to learn grape growing, but it was not meant to be.

New Life at Shoalhaven Heads

Shoalhaven Heads is on the south coast of NSW, surrounded by farmlands with long, open, sandy beaches stretching nearly 12 kilometres. A very beautiful place to live. Land was selling quickly in the new subdivisions near the beach. Mum and Dad were excited to build a new house there and be able to choose the colour schemes and designs to suit their early retirement.

They moved into their new brick three-bedroom bungalow at 8 Boyd Street, Shoalhaven Heads. Mum and Dad loved their new home, painting the interior walls a light blue. The kitchen was blue and white, their favourite colour scheme. The garden was a large flat blank canvas and Dad quickly got to work on designing flower beds, pathways, vegetable patches, herb gardens and a pergola for morning tea or a barbeque. Mark helped Dad put up his wooden paling fences one weekend so they could get a dog.

Dad soon had his garden full of flowers, herbs, and vegetables. I never understood his passion for gardening back then, but 30 years later, I really do get his enthusiasm for growing food and flowers. Maybe it is a mature person's pastime, but I love growing my own herbs, vegetables and fruit. I am very lucky to live in a climate that makes it incredibly easy to grow almost anything.

New house, new dog. I bought a mature female black cocker spaniel called "Misty" from a family in Mudgee. Mum and Dad enjoyed taking her for daily walks. Strangely, this dog had a bad odour even after a good bath, but was so loyal, she was always following Dad around. In the garden, she would sit right behind him, never too far away. This was one of Dad's most favourite pastimes, gardening with a dog by his side. As I reflect on this, it must be a Hinchcliffe thing because I love gardening too with my dog, Oscar, always by my side.

Being retired, Dad had plenty of time to potter around the garden but had to take it slow, as his back pain was still crippling at times. His back surgery didn't completely fix his pain. He joined the local swimming pool and would swim his laps religiously summer and winter in the outdoor local swimming pool. Swimming was one of the activities that would not antagonize his back. Dad loved the great outdoors, going for walks to the beach and along the river. The flat terrain of Shoalhaven Heads made it much easier for walking on level surfaces.

Mum and Dad were in their 50s, where the neighbours behind them seemed elderly, but were probably only in their 60s. They were very friendly. Mum and Dad liked them a lot, often chatting over the adjoining fence. Mum made friends with a lady across the road and often had morning tea with her.

As Dad was no longer the breadwinner, Mum found work at Kiama Nursing Home as an assistant nurse. She didn't stay long because she soon discovered it wasn't a good place to work. Financially, it was a difficult time for Dad, not being able to access a pension until he used up his superannuation. Being in his early 50s, he was 10 plus years too young for an aged pension. These days, he would have been entitled to a disability pension as the surgery had decreased his ability to work as a labourer and he still suffered ongoing back pain.

Mum's health soon deteriorated, with all her worry about Dad's pain and their livelihood. She had her first episode of an obstructed bowel. She was rushed to the hospital in Berry. Her pain was extreme. By lucky coincidence, Mark and I were visiting that weekend from Mudgee. I sat in the back seat holding her tightly while Mark drove with Dad in the passenger's seat next to him.

Mum stayed at Berry Hospital overnight, then the following day was transferred to Nowra Hospital for emergency bowel surgery. We all were totally shocked to see her so ill, thankfully she did eventually recover.

When I was 25-years-old, my marriage ended, and we chose to go our separate ways. We had been together for over 10 years, since we were teenagers at school. In November 1989, we sold our beautiful farm and gave our horses away. I quit my office job at Mudgee Hospital so I could flee back to Wollongong to be near family.

Thankfully, I was able to stay with John and Evelyne in their granny flat until I found my feet again. An old college friend got me a weekend job in a nursing home. A few months later, I gave myself a four-week holiday treat and trekked the high altitudes of the Himalaya Mountains in Nepal. After my holiday, I was able to get a full-time contract office job at BHP Steel, Port Kembla, where I made a lot of new friendships. This contract ended up lasting six years. Working full-time, I was able to move into a shared flat in Wollongong renting with a university student, Djahida, who became a good friend still to this day.

In May 1990, Mum and Dad travelled to Dubbo, to help if needed, for the pending birth of their next grandchild. They got there just in time as Paul took ill and was rushed into hospital, ultimately requiring emergency bowel surgery. He was diagnosed with Crohn's disease. At one stage both Paul and Deborah were recovering respectively from surgery and birthing in Dubbo Base Hospital. Mum and Dad were able to take care of a young eight-year-old Peter while his

Mummy and Daddy were in hospital. Their fourth grandchild, Emma, was born to Paul and Deborah in May 1990.

The itchy feet kicked in again with Mum and Dad unable to settle into an early retirement. It wasn't long before Dad decided they needed a LONG holiday, six months. They moved back to England for an extended holiday after selling their newly built house at Shoalhaven Heads. Upon arrival back in Australia, they were able to move into John and Evelyne's granny flat at Albion Park Rail. Mum and Dad decided to rebuild at Shoalhaven Heads, this time for good. No looking back.

My first Christmas after leaving Mudgee, Mum, Dad, Paul and family came to my flat in Wollongong for Christmas lunch. Dad had his religious 40 winks rest on my bed with baby Emma. On Christmas evening, we all went to John and Evelyne's house for a lovely evening meal and party with their young family. Both John and Evelyne loved cooking and entertaining. Evelyne has French-Italian heritage and her meals were always exquisitely delicious. John prided himself on his cooking, too. I loved going to their house.

My dear friend, Mary, passed away after her long battle with cancer. I had worked with Mary at Mudgee Hospital; she was like an older sister to me. I felt the need to go to her funeral. Dad came with me and we stayed overnight in Mudgee. It was nice to catch up with a couple of old farm neighbours and friends, but it was very sad at her funeral. I cried at her grave site when the coffin was lowered into the ground and felt embarrassed to be consoled by Mary's husband. I was grateful Dad had accompanied me to Mudgee that difficult weekend. He was always very caring, kind and protective of me, even then, when I felt totally grown up at 26 years of age.

Mum and Dad re-built a new bungalow at 61 Scott Street, Shoalhaven Heads. This time, they chose a new colour scheme. They decided on mostly apricot and white with a dark green feature wall in the bathroom. It was a lovely three-bedroom home on a very large 722sqm corner block of land with extra side access. Another blank canvas for Dad to get in and design his garden beds from scratch. Dad continued his long walks to the beach, river and swimming at the swimming pool. The local shops and bowling club were only a 15-minute walk away.

New house, new dog. This time I bought Mum and Dad a puppy. It was a blue cattle dog. The puppy loved biting everyone's heels, especially while hanging out the clothes on the washing line. He was a very energetic little pup. Unfortunately, he had a very short life and died from tick paralysis. It was very sad to lose him so young.

Once settled into their new home, they decided to start their own cleaning business. Mum was 55 and Dad was 57-years-old. My three flatmates and I were their first customers. We were renting a large four-bedroom house in Figtree, near Wollongong. The word soon spread to our work colleagues. There was zero advertising required; it was all word of mouth, ending up with quite a few regular jobs each week.

I felt they always went above and beyond what was expected to be cleaned. One day my next-door neighbour mentioned to me, "the cleaners even got into your pool to scrub the edges". Yes, that was Dad scrubbing the dirt or mould, off the side of the pool. We were very lucky. I'm sure they spent more hours cleaning than most of us realised. Being young, carefree adults, we would rush around at the last-minute tidying up our rooms before they arrived to clean. It was usually on Fridays. Mum and Dad worked hard all morning, then stopped for a late lunch of either takeaway fish and chips or popped into the Returned Services Leagues (RSL) club for a meal before heading home. It was about a 30 to 45-minute drive away to Shoalhaven Heads.

I used to ride horses most weekends at the Foxground Riding School, south of Kiama. I was a confident rider, having had my own horses to ride in Mudgee. One eventful Sunday ride, I opted not to wear a helmet because it was a sunny day. I wore my Akubra hat for shade over my face. As we rode towards the stables, after a very slow ride with a large group of beginner riders, my friend Djahida and I decided to have a bit of a gallop with the permission of the riding school leader. We rode across an unfamiliar paddock, not knowing our exact location too well, then the horses just took off. We couldn't pull them up and a fence was fast approaching us. My competitive friend thought I was racing her, and that I knew the way. The only option was to turn left to avoid hitting the fence, and we both went down an embankment with our horses. I landed on my head knocking me out. An ambulance arrived quickly and I was flown via helicopter from Nowra Hospital to a Sydney hospital. Djahida got out of it with only an injured wrist. She went to my parent's house to tell them about the accident, because there were no mobile phones then.

I awoke in Intensive Care Unit (ICU) 18 hours later to the smiling reassuring faces of both Evelyne and John. The following day, the doctors told me that my scans also revealed a benign brain tumour, the size of a golf ball on my frontal cortex. The neurosurgeon wanted to remove it in eight weeks after the head injury healed. I had a gash in the back of my head, and still to this day, I have a skull indent and scar.

After a lot of my own healing work, including visualisation and spiritual, psychic healing from family and friends, my tumour had dissolved by the time I had my second lot of scans six weeks after the riding accident. The neurosurgeon examined my second lot of scans and was gob-smacked. He pointed to the earlier scan with the tumour and then to the new scan—now with no tumour visible.

My husband and wife team of general practitioners were thrilled with my outcome. They were very supportive and I am grateful for their kindness in my time of great need for reassurance. The tumour healing was certainly a big message of hope and miracles. It has given me a lived experience and awareness of how powerful our bodies are at healing themselves within the right environment. This event changed the course of my life forever. Being able to heal the seemingly impossible can be possible.

Reflecting on how people react when faced with frightening health or emotional issues, my brother John was always upbeat. He never for a moment thought that my brain tumour would become a problem for me and would often tease me with his weird sense of humour.

Christmas that year was worth celebrating on many levels. Our entire family was able to get to Mum and Dad's new home for Christmas. All the family arrived on Christmas Day, including my new boyfriend, Gary.

It was a hot summer's day but cool enough with all the fans going to drink plenty of iced cold beers. Dad had put up long trestle tables in the garage so all 12 of us could be seated for a traditional English Christmas meal. He was especially proud of his newly built home with plenty of flowers, herbs and vegetables growing in the garden beds.

On Boxing Day, I moved into Gary's house at 15 Porter Street, North Wollongong. Gary carried me over the threshold. We were both very excited for a new beginning together, officially.

Much to our delight, Paul and his family moved to Kiama, a 20-minute drive north of Shoalhaven Heads. Paul had a new opportunity with his work as the bank manager for the Kiama branch. We were all thrilled to have Paul and his family finally living near us, expecting to have many more family gatherings on weekends.

Dad loved our Hinchcliffe Christmas party at Paul's house the following year. Both Deborah and Gary had the task of making the Christmas cocktails. The grandchildren played with their new walkie-talkies on the verandah that overlooked the ocean and beaches down the valley. Evelyne arrived a little later, after finishing her shift at work. Mum and John enjoyed showing the grandkids how to jump on the trampoline. It was a lovely day with the Hinchcliffe tribe.

In the early 1990s, Dad was diagnosed with blocked arteries. He had a stent inserted into his artery at the St Vincent's Heart Health Hospital in Sydney. My old flatmate Djahida was an exercise scientist in the cardiology department and made several visits to check in on Dad during her work shifts after his surgery. He was really pleased to see a familiar face who understood his ordeal. It was around this time that Mum discovered she had breast cancer. Her cancer was removed with a lumpectomy followed by radiotherapy, and it never came back, having been over 20 years now.

Dad's birthday was on the 10th of February and mine was on the 16th, so we decided to combine his 60th and my 30th celebrations. Both my family and Gary's family, along with many friends, made it quite a big party combining our 90 years. The party was in our backyard at Porter Street, Wollongong. We hired a caterer for a spit roast and lots of salads. There were a couple of gazebos in the garden for shade that sheltered us from the heat of the summer sun. It was a lovely way to celebrate our birthday milestones.

One year later, I married Gary, on the 11th of February 1995 at Wollongong Lighthouse. Dad was really pleased that I was now making plans to settle down by getting married. He liked Gary and approved of his ex-military credentials, having been in the Army Reserves and the Police Force before we got married. The unspoken respect and camaraderie amongst the military community is unwavering. He could see that Gary had a protective nature to always look out for me.

Much to everyone's sadness, John had recently ended his marriage to Evelyne, and they sold their family home at Albion Park Rail. John moved to Wollongong and rented a flat near the beach and continued to work at Helensburgh Pit. Evelyne moved into her flat in Fairy Meadow, not far away, with their girls. John and Evelyne remained good friends. Paul also moved away from Kiama for career advancement to Lismore, northwestern NSW, then later into Brisbane, over the border into Queensland.

After twelve months of marriage I wasn't pregnant, so Dad thought we weren't going to have any children. He felt I was happily settled, and it was time for them to live the life they desired in retirement. Us kids were mature adults; I was 32, John 38 and Paul 40. England was beckoning; they wanted to enjoy their golden years in their homeland, so they made the decision to relocate. They sold their home at Shoalhaven Heads for the second time.

Relocation to Folkestone (1996)

The pull to English culture was strong. Mum's proviso was they had to be in Folkestone, living near her parents and her sisters, Joy, Barbara and Mary. They couldn't have got any closer, buying a house just 12 doors down the road from Barbara, with Joy only one street away. Mum's parents and Mary were only a short drive away in Dover. They were both so happy to be back in Kent.

Their new home was a three-level terrace house, 46 Linden Crescent. Downstairs was a living-dining room and kitchen, the next level—a bathroom, a couple steps to a bedroom that they made into a sewing room, a few more steps up to the master bedroom, then more steps up to the attic large guest bedroom. Dad put in a wooden garden shed, barbeque patio area, and lots of flowers in the back garden. They completely renovated this house with new carpet, fresh paint, a new kitchen (blue and white) and a lovely blue stove. Mum put up lace curtains, and they had the house looking perfectly British.

Dad bought a fax machine soon after moving in. This enabled them to write faxes to us kids daily. On the bottom of their faxed messages, he drew comical characters and scenes describing their day. It was only then that I realised how good Dad was at drawing. I have kept many of his faxes by photocopying them off the wax fax paper before they faded. In those days, using a fax machine was a very quick and inexpensive way to send daily letters overseas. Today we could compare it to Facebook, Messenger or text messages on our phones.

Mum and Dad both enjoyed walking as much as possible around Folkestone to the shops or harbour. In good weather, they often walked from Folkestone to Hythe (eight kilometres one way) or Folkestone to Dover (12 kilometres one way), hiking along the cliff tops or walking along the coastline promenades for day trips out. They usually caught a bus back. Long distance walking was a favourite pastime. Paul has continued with that family gene of long-distance hikes. He was 63-years-old when he completed the Kokoda challenge in 33 hours. It is a 96 kilometre overnight and day trek through the Gold Coast Hinterland.

Dad was registered with the East Kent Grenadier Guard Association. He loved attending the regular local meetings and helping on market day stalls for the association.

Dad and Jimmy first met as school children (in the same class) and later caught up in the Grenadier Guards as young men. When Dad moved back to England in 1996, he met up with Jimmy yet again. This time Jimmy was running souvenir shops in both Deal and Folkestone. Dad ended up working with Jimmy at "Pandora's Box" in the Old High Street of Folkestone and sometimes went to London with Jimmy to the warehouses sourcing stock for his shops. They both had a sense of humour and laughed a lot like brothers. Dad loved working a couple of days weekly in Jimmy's Folkestone shop.

With Dad working at Pandora's Box, Mum decided to do some volunteer work in a local charity shop. Being in their mid-60s both Mum and Dad still had the energy and drive to be working a few days weekly. It kept them in touch with their community at a pace they could still appreciate in their retired lifestyle.

Thankfully, Mum and Dad travelled back to Australia for an extended holiday of two months to support me with the birth of my first child. The fifth grandchild, George, was born in November 1998. Both Mum and Gary were in the birthing suite at Figtree Private Hospital to witness the birth. That evening when I finally got to bed to sleep, I felt a gentle hand placed on the side of my face. I believe it was my Grandma Hinchcliffe's hand of reassurance.

Mum and Dad stayed with our new little family until Boxing Day. Gary was away at work for up to 10 days at a time, being an international flight attendant. So, it was wonderful to have Mum and Dad's support for my early weeks of motherhood.

We had a beautiful Christmas Day at home with the Hinchcliffe tribe. Having such a young baby, I felt like I was constantly breastfeeding or changing nappies. I was grateful to have my family to help me. On Boxing Day, Paul, John and I had ordered a surprise limousine car to take Mum and Dad back to Sydney airport for their flight home. There were many goodbye tears as they climbed into the limousine.

Gary had two back-to-back London trips on his work roster, so I took this opportunity to take George with me and fly on Gary's trips. The staff travel perks were of great benefit. I was so excited to see Mum and Dad with six-month-old George. We travelled on Gary's flights, being very well looked after by the flight crew. We caught a train from London down to Folkestone to be met at the train station by a very happy Dad. I had two weeks to enjoy a brief holiday before Gary returned to London for his second work flight back to Australia.

I was ready to show George off to meet his extended English family. There were cousins, great aunties and great-grandparents to meet. Mum and Dad were thrilled to have us stay in their new Linden Crescent home. The guest bedroom was in the large attic, being tastefully decorated with lemon painted walls and light blue decorations. It was very comfortable for George and me. Just eating Mum and Dad's meals again was a holiday for me.

Most days we would be either visiting relatives or going for country drives, stopping at quaint English pubs in picturesque villages. George got his first trip to France. At the time there were one-pound ferry day trips to Calais and Boulogne in France, so we took George on his first ferry ride across the English Channel.

Both to and from London, we had stopovers in Bangkok, Thailand. George was idolised in Bangkok. They loved his blue eyes, fair skin and caramel blonde hair. Many wanted to touch him as we walked down the city streets. I felt a little nervous, but Gary usually carried him close to his chest in a firm grip hold. The young Thai women loved holding George while I had my nails done in a salon. He didn't seem to mind. He was a great little traveller and loved all the stranger's cuddles and attention.

Dad bought a car in England. He drove for a further two years but eventually found the roads too busy. Simply getting a park outside his house was very difficult. He decided to sell his car at aged 65 and then handed in his license.

After I left England, it was not long before I found out I was pregnant again. Mum was already missing her youngest grandchild, George, but now there was a new family member on his way. The dilemma of being with her grandchildren and children versus staying in England near her sisters and parents was very difficult. Her heart strings were being pulled in both directions. Dad loved his new English house, working with his best friend Jimmy in his shop, attending the meetings with the Grenadier Guards Association, long countryside walks, English pubs, the English culture and all the familiar places he had grown up in. It was a tough decision to leave it all behind again.

60th plus 30th Birthday Party for Arnold and Alison, Australia.

Arnold having a tea break, in the woods, Kent, England.

East Kent Branch, Grenadier Guards Association, market day stall.

Alison Simpson

11
THE TRAVELLING NOMADS

Australia calls (2000)

In early 2000, Mum and Dad sold their newly renovated English terrace house in Linden Crescent within weeks of it going on the market. Having spent a lot of money doing up the house, they sold it at a good price, making a little profit. The lady who bought their house opted to have some of their furniture, which helped them with less moving costs back to Australia. This time, they moved back to Australia with some of their furniture and possessions in a container sent by sea.

Mum and Dad moved in with us for the upcoming birth of their next grandchild. When it was time for me to go to hospital, I literally threw toddler George into Mum's arms as Gary and I rushed out the door, quickly scrambling into the car. Harry arrived safely, being delivered in hospital within one hour of pulling up in the car park. Coincidentally, he was born in the same labour room and enjoyed the same hospital suite, room 44, that had a view of the paddock of horses, which I experienced with George 17 months earlier. The sixth grandchild was born, Harry, in April 2000, our second baby boy.

Not knowing where they may end up, Dad felt he didn't want to buy again as they had bought and sold too many times already. He suggested Gary and I buy a unit that they could rent from us. We bought a two-bedroom unit in Grey Street, Keiraville, near Wollongong Botanical Gardens.

It was a lovely flat. Dad quickly got to work planting flowers to dress up the small garden in front of their verandah. He updated the bathroom, putting in a lovely new English styled vanity unit and new dusty pink tiling. They had the flat looking comfortable with an English cottage flair.

Mum and Dad bought their first computer. This is when Dad started to take an interest in writing his autobiography. Paul typed as Dad recounted his memories from birth until he was 37-years-old. Mum loved the computer, too. I nicknamed her "Granny Graphics", as she had so much fun creating graphics and writing letters back to her sisters and parents. She was very quick at picking up on how to do things on the computer. The computer became a fun pastime for them both in their second bedroom. To this day, mum at 85 years old, still enjoys writing emails on her computer.

The flat was a short walk, up a steep hill, to the local shops. It took them about 45 minutes to walk to the main shops in Wollongong or the Wollongong beaches. Dad enjoyed swimming again, doing laps at the open sea Continental Baths at Wollongong Beach. I lived a good 30-minute walk away in an easterly direction towards the beach from their new flat.

Paul, John and I gave Mum and Dad a luxury weekend away at the Rocks in Sydney, for their 45th Wedding Anniversary. The Rocks is an area near Sydney Harbour which overlooks the Sydney Opera House and Circular Quay, where huge cruise liners and ferries come and go. The Rocks is an older, quaint part of Sydney, with cobbled street lanes filled with exclusive shops and restaurants. We booked them into the luxurious Rydges Hotel.

For their anniversary dinner, Gary and I booked them into the Hofbrauhouse German Restaurant, now known as the Munich Brauhaus. I remember walking into this restaurant to reserve the best table, making sure the Maitra d' knew it was their 45th Wedding Anniversary. I was extremely happy that Mum and Dad reported having a very special time at this restaurant. The Maitra d' and staff looked after them from the minute they walked in to the moment they left the restaurant.

On the morning of their hotel check out, Gary and I met them in the foyer. Mum's face was radiantly glowing. She looked so relaxed and content. Mum happily told us the hotel supplied bath robes to wear to the rooftop swimming pool that overlooked the harbour. She recounted the weekend had been wonderful. Dad said they had been treated like royalty both at the hotel and in the restaurant. How beautiful for them both. Only the best for my parents.

George and Harry were in a double pram. Mum and Dad often took them for pram rides and park play times at the Botanical Garden with picnics when I was teaching fitness classes. Harry developed a Yorkshire accent when he was a toddler. It was noticeable if he'd spent a day with Dad, as Dad would teach him the Yorkshire accent, words, and phrases.

The Queen's Invitation

Still being registered with the Grenadier Guards Association, Dad and Mum were invited to Buckingham Palace to meet the Queen and Prince Phillip for high tea. Being invited to the palace was a very good reason to have another holiday in England. Dad took up the invitation to meet the Queen, but Mum declined the offer, being too shy to meet royalty.

"Had a lovely day at Buckingham Palace today. It was very hot. We entered upon a red-carpet walking from the front of the palace to the back of the palace. We had cakes and sandwiches, then the Queen came out at four o'clock. She walked and talked to a lot of

people, and so did Prince Phillip. I really enjoyed it. It would have been better if it had not been so hot". (Dad's diary entry on the 26th of July 2000).

Coast-to-coast Walk

Dad always dreamed of doing England's coast to coast walk of 293 kilometres because he just loved walking and the English countryside. This long walk starts at St Bees on the west coast of England, finishing on the east coast at Robin Hood Bay.

Excitingly, they filled their huge backpacks with all their holiday trekking gear and caught a train at 9.30am from Dover. Three trains and one taxi later, they arrived at St Bees at 7pm feeling very weary. "What can we get rid of?" asked Mum, trying to repack their overloaded backpacks at their guest house for the night.

The following morning, after a lovely big breakfast, they set off bright and early at 7.30am. Along the way, Dad lost his walking stick, having put it down when they stopped for a cuppa and not picked it up again when they walked off. After a one-hour detour to retrace their steps, they found his walking stick, enabling them to get back on the right path. They wearily reached Ennerdale after seven hours of walking, with plenty of rest stops along the way.

It was another hot and sunny day of pleasant walking on level terrain before they arrived at a Youth Hostel to refill their water bottles with cool water and use their toilets. However, the mood soon changed when Mum saw a very steep mountain ahead. She thought they would walk around it somehow—not go up it.

The mountain had loose stones, and they had to grab the heather flora to pull themselves upwards, literally on their hands and knees, to climb their first mountain. At one flattened area, they rested and fell asleep for some 40 winks. After their nap, they pulled themselves together, onwards and upwards, and continued to the top of the mountain. Mum says the descent was not much easier, having to gingerly watch each step to prevent falling. Finally reaching their guesthouse for the night, Dad discovered his knees were in bad shape and Mum's foot was swollen. Mum's diary entry says it all: *"Emmerdale to Borrowdale; What a day we have had, it nearly killed us. We didn't realise that we had to climb a mountain. There was no other way."*

The following morning after breakfast, they decided not to continue with their walk across England as they just weren't well enough. They walked along the road hoping to catch a bus. To their luck, an open top double-decker bus to Keswick came past at 10am. They sat at the top of the bus, relaxing as they enjoyed the scenery of the English countryside going to Keswick. Arriving in Keswick, they found themselves a nice guest house for the night. The following day, they did a bit of washing and caught a bus to Ambleside and back to Keswick.

"We had a one and half-hour trip round the lake. It was a lovely day. Took some lovely photos after the trip. We walked round the Beatrix Potter Place after a few hours in Windermere. We caught the bus on to Kendal. We only spent an hour and half walking around shops." (Dad's diary entry on 2nd August 2000).

"Left the guest house, decided to travel by bus to Penrith then on to Carlisle, but reaching Carlisle the weather was so bad and the place looked so dull we decided to go to the railway station and get the next train to Dover. Left Carlisle at one o'clock, arrived back in Dover at nine at night. Train to London was fast. Lovely trains. As the train was late, I was allowed to phone from the train. They would tell you what train you could get next to continue your journey home." (Dad's diary entry on 3rd August 2000).

Mum and Dad enjoyed their holiday in England. Even though they didn't complete the coast-to-coast walk, it was an adventure.

I had a personal training studio set up in the old front living room of our house so I could work from home whilst looking after toddler George and baby Harry. Mum and Dad planned a holiday on the Queen Elizabeth (QE2) Cruise Ship, so Mum was keen to get fit and trim for their cruising holiday.

I loved coaching Mum with her exercise routines. She was extremely co-ordinated, bringing back all her happy school memories when she was proficient at gymnastics. Dad had a highly disciplined nature and was able to support her by encouraging only healthy foods and going on a lot of long walks. Mum's before and after photos were incredible. To me, she looked younger and fitter than I had ever seen her before. She was a very fit 66-year-old. She bought a beautiful burgundy silk and lace evening gown to wear on the QE2, in a size 14, but by the time she was ready to go, it had to be taken in by a dressmaker to a glamorous size 12.

QE2 World Cruise (2002)

Mum and Dad booked their well-deserved holiday of a lifetime, as they both loved ocean travel. It included airfares to Singapore, then travelling on the luxurious QE2 all the way to England (32 nights) via many ports of call and flights home to Sydney. They paid $9674 per person, and said it was worth every penny and more.

On Saturday 16th March 2002, Gary, George and Harry called by wishing Mum and Dad well for their trip, seeing them onto the airport shuttle bus to Sydney airport. John and Claire met up with them at Sydney airport for some much needed Bon voyage drinks before their flight to Singapore. The Queen Elizabeth II Ship was docked in Singapore Harbour, due to depart on the 17th of March 2002 for the world cruise to England.

Singapore

Arriving in Singapore, they had an overnight stay at the luxurious Marina Mandarin Hotel, on Raffles Boulevarde. With only a short stay in Singapore, they headed to the iconic Raffles Hotel Long Bar for a gin-based cocktail, the Singapore Sling. This cocktail was created in 1915 by a bartender who worked at the Long Bar of Raffles Hotel.

Raffles Hotel first opened in 1887, and in 1987, the government gave it the heritage monument title. It is a must-see for all tourists going to Singapore. With Gary and six-month-old baby George, I had my first trip to Singapore. No Singapore Sling for me as I was still breastfeeding, so we settled for breakfast at the old worldly cafe and bakery of Raffles Hotel. In 2004, we were all back there. This time, it was Harry's first visit to Raffles Hotel, a stopover on our way to England for a holiday.

Between 1 to 3pm on Sunday 17th March, Mum and Dad boarded the QE2 from Singapore Harbour. Mum says the ship was extremely big, being quite worried they wouldn't find their way around and get lost. Yes, they did get lost several times on the first day or two.

First things first, they unpacked their clothes and set up their room for the next 32 nights, sailing across the oceans. Soon after arriving on board, all the passengers had to do a boat drill, putting on their life jackets and walking to their designated locations.

Their first meal was in the Lido, a self-serve restaurant for dinner. Here the dress code was casual, but Mum felt it was still very posh. She noted there were beautiful green tablecloths and napkins. After dinner they had a look around the ship as if they were on an expedition, but by 9pm they headed back to their cabin for 40 winks, awaking two hours later. The ship was still in the port of Singapore, so they got themselves a drink on deck to watch the ship depart Singapore at 12.45am. That night, they had enjoyed cocktails with the Captain and the other 648 new arrival passengers that boarded the ship in Singapore.

To maintain their fitness, they walked at least five kilometres around the ship before breakfast every day, followed by a swim and spa. Dad always liked using the stairs to keep them both fit so they could really enjoy the wonderful food and drinks available to them. He was very regimented about maintaining his fitness.

Mum says, when they were having dinner, the cabin attendants turned down the sheets, preparing their bedding with immaculate precision. Mum's nightie was spread out into a fan shape with a chocolate on it. Everything was done so beautifully they felt like royalty. Sitting by the window having a drink, Mum and Dad started planning their trips for their next port of call, India.

Cochin (Kochi) Port - India

Cochin is a major port city of southern India known for its 16th century churches, synagogue and fort from the earlier colonial inhabitants, Portuguese, Dutch and English. It was a very hot, humid day for Mum and Dad's first port of call in India. It was 34 degrees Celsius with 84 percent humidity.

Mum wrote: *"It was very sad to see how poor these Indians are. The beggars really made me feel bad. I would have liked to give away all my money to them. We were shown a few churches and then a walk down an awful street. There were a lot of little shops, but we weren't allowed to stop as we had to catch a ferry back to the ship for lunch, where everyone was waited on, hand and foot."*

Mum and Dad did their usual walking laps around the ship, but Mum did an extra two laps, followed by a swim and spa before their breakfast by the pool. Mum decided she would try the exercise class at 10am. She met a northern English woman at the class who showed her the ropes. Prior to joining the cruise, Mum had been personally trained in my home gym studio, so she found this class to be very easy, but still she really enjoyed it as the exercises were synchronised to music like a dance class.

At 11am, Dad met Mum in the theatre for a talk on the Royal Family history by Hugo Vickers. Mum dropped off to sleep several times during the talk, but Dad loved this topic and was wide awake throughout.

Whilst enjoying a refreshing pint before lunch, they watched a dart's match. Apparently, not many people knew how to throw the darts, so Mum and Dad decided to join the next match, to show them how it was done.

They found it was easy to strike up conversations, as many people were willing to have a nice old chat. Everyone seemed quite friendly, happily sharing their life stories.

Mumbai, India

Mum and Dad had a port of call into Mumbai where they travelled on a morning coach tour. Mumbai is India's largest city, densely populated with over 12 million people. This is India's financial centre and the heart of the film industry, Bollywood. Mumbai was formerly known as Bombay until 1995. Many other cities in India have been de-anglicised, renaming them in keeping with their own Indian heritage.

"We were shocked at all the beggars, thin, little women, men and children, sometimes crippled. It was awful to see. When we got off the coach to look at anything, they would crowd around you. Arnold and I didn't like it." (Mum's diary)

India was Mum's first exposure to seeing poverty firsthand. Dad had come across impoverished cultures during his Merchant Navy and Army tours, but it didn't make it any easier for him to witness again. They were pleased to be back on the ship at 1pm.

After lunch on the QE2, it was time for a swim and a sunbath by the pool, but they found it too hot to stay long. Off they went to explore the upper decks and found a nice area in the shade to lie on deck chairs. Falling asleep for well over an hour, Mum said afternoon tea was being served and Dad was still snoring away happily in his deck chair. In the evening, they headed to the Grand Lounge to listen to a comedian, John Martin, who was so funny they simply laughed their heads off, said Mum.

Dressed in their finery, Mum wearing her beautiful burgundy silk and lace evening gown along with Dad wearing his black dinner suit with a black bow tie, they headed to dinner in the posh Mauretania Restaurant on Upper Deck.

Feeling so glamorous, Mum wanted to have the QE2 photographers take a photo of them both. Dad was shy about having an official photograph, as there was quite an audience watching. Dad's motto was, "Happy wife—happy life", and she persuaded him to get a photo. The following day, after collecting the photo, they were thrilled they had made the effort. It was a great photo and a wonderful keepsake to treasure.

After a posh dinner, Mum and Dad listened to Petula Clark performing. She was in her late 60s and still had a fabulous voice. They especially enjoyed her hit song *Downtown*, which was released in 1964.

Next, they headed to the Queens Lounge, which was decorated with the theme of "A song of India". Many women had bought their own Indian Sari dresses, and some men had turbans on with Indian costumes. They watched the Indian dancing for as long as they could before heading to their cabin at 11pm, after a wonderful evening out.

It was time for the QE2 ship to cross the equator, so King Neptune came aboard for the equator crossing ceremony. Passengers were invited to take part in this ceremony. Dad offered to participate while Mum filmed him. He was dunked under the water in the pool by King Neptune, an equatorial baptism.

King Neptune was originally from the Roman religion, being a God of freshwater. By 399BC he evolved into becoming the God of all seas, earthquakes and horses in Greek mythology. King Neptune is a merman with a long woolly beard holding a trident spear often depicted seated in a seashell drawn by seahorses.

Victoria on Mahe Island, Seychelles

The QE2 stopped at Victoria on Mahe Island, Seychelles, which is situated in the Indian Ocean. There are over 100 islands of lush tropical vegetation and silver-white sandy beaches in Seychelles. Mum and Dad took a 20-minute choppy sea launch to Victoria from the ship. It was another very hot day. They were able to walk into the main town to explore the shops and found a cafe to recover with a nice drink. It was a colourful place but also expensive; a hair clip cost $16 and two cheap t-shirts were $56. Being such a hot day, they took a taxi to a beautiful tropical beach, which was stunning.

Many other QE2 passengers were on the beach along with QE2 young staff, enjoying a break from working. In the evening, a group of dancers boarded the ship to perform a traditional dance from the Seychelles. Dad filmed the colourfully dressed dancers performing.

As I read Mum's travel diary, the lifestyle of walking, swimming, exploring ports and eating in beautiful restaurants makes me so jealous. Wow! I've never considered a cruise before, but maybe I should put this on my bucket list. I will be in my 60s soon.

Mum and Dad joined another darts match. This time there were 33 players. Not wanting to boast but Mum came sixth out of the 33 players, not knowing how to play. She thought it was purely good luck. Dad did well. He scored 78 but was knocked out by a man who scored 98. The following day, they joined another darts match. Lucky Mum threw the last winning dart and won a prize for that match. Dad's mother used to play darts regularly in her day. It was a very popular pastime in English pubs in the 1930s.

The next port of call was Mauritius on the east coast of Africa.

Mauritius, East Africa

Arriving at the Port Louis, the capital of Mauritius, they went ashore on a small boat and started walking towards the shops. Meeting up with another passenger, 79-year-old Len, the three of them decided to hire a taxi and explore the island together. The taxi driver was about 25-years-old and took them all over the island, stopping many times for them to take photos and do some shopping.

They were driven to the Mauritius National Botanical Garden. These gardens are now considered to be the oldest botanical gardens in the southern hemisphere. Further, they were taken to the serene beach of Mont Choisy, where the driver waited while they went for a swim. It was a very enjoyable morning out with the taxi driver/tour guide. Back on the ship in the afternoon, they watched from the deck as they left Port Louis, Mauritius.

Fifteen days into their cruise, Mum and Dad decided to weigh themselves. To their amazement, they hadn't put on any weight after two weeks of cruising. They were thrilled to have kept up their daily exercise and not overeat, a miraculous achievement. When they arrived back at their cabin, a basket of Easter eggs were gifted to them from the QE2, being Easter Sunday. It was a delightful service where nothing was left to chance. No wonder they felt like royalty on their world cruise.

Dad surprised Mum by renewing their wedding vows in the presence of the QE2 Captain and a QE2 Celebrant on the 1st of April 2002. Not aware of how formal the ceremony would be, they put on their smart, casual clothes. Other couples were in more formal attire. Mum was wearing her blue and white striped sundress and Dad had a nice collared light blue shirt and cream shorts. Both looked amazingly healthy, fit, tanned, and happy. To end this perfect day, they went to dinner in the posh restaurant Mauretania to celebrate, followed by a show in the Grand Lounge.

Durban, South Africa

The ship docked in the busy harbour city of Durban, the chief seaport of South Africa. Mum and Dad had booked their shore adventure to meet the Zulu people on a plateau high up in the hills overlooking the deep valleys below. The Zulus welcomed them to their land and offered them a traditional dancing performance for the QE2 passengers. Following the dancing, the passengers were invited to have photos taken with the Zulu people. Mum says they were very friendly and really enjoyed having their photos taken.

Mum and Dad noticed their fitness improved because their daily walks were getting much quicker, so they had to extend the distances. Mum also kept up her daily exercise classes. Dad would encourage Mum to use the stairs rather than lifts whenever possible. On many mornings, they would be up before the sun came up to do their daily walks.

Cape Town, South Africa

Arriving in Cape Town, it was pouring with rain, so the Tabletop Mountain cable car was out of action due to wet weather. The Tabletop Mountain rises 1,084m above sea level, having an expansive view across the entire city of Cape Town. The plateau on top of the mountain is a perfect viewing deck for photography.

Instead, Mum and Dad decided to take a bus tour visiting museums, beaches, and shops. Ready for something to eat, they found a lovely cafe and invited a couple of fellow QE2 passengers to share a table, enjoying a good chat over lunch together.

The following day, Dad was determined to visit the Tabletop Mountain, the most popular tourist attraction in Cape Town. This time, they caught a taxi directly to the elevated plateau. The driver was happy to wait while they took photographs and videos of the view.

The next tourist spot was the Two Oceans Aquarium, but this time, the taxi driver didn't wait. The aquarium was well known for its diverse aquatic species from both the Indian and Atlantic Oceans.

After that, a taxi took them to the Castle of Good Hope. The timing was perfect as they had a chance to watch the Changing of the Guards, something Dad loved to see, being an old Guardsman himself. This castle was built between 1666 and 1679 and is the oldest building in South Africa. Mum and Dad enjoyed lunch at the castle, then walked out to look for a taxi ride to the shops, but to their surprise, the driver had waited for them that entire time.

Back on board the QE2, and the ship set sail at 6pm for St Helena. Mum and Dad were both looking forward to getting to Southampton, England, having been at sea for three weeks.

Saint Helena Island, Atlantic Ocean

The next port of call was Rupert's Bay in Saint Helena Island. This island is completely isolated, situated in the middle of the Atlantic Ocean, 2000 kilometres west of Africa. It is a British governed outpost where Napoleon Bonaparte was exiled. He lived there for six years before he died in 1821. Dad had been to Saint Helena when he was in the Merchant Navy.

They took the launch boat from the QE2 to the island to do a little souvenir shopping in Jamestown and join a three-hour bus tour. The tour took them to see where Napoleon lived and his burial site, followed by where the current Governor General lives on the island. Steep mountains overhang the township. There were 699 vertically steep steps to the top of the escarpment overlooking Rupert's Bay. Mum and Dad were very glad to be on a bus tour and not attempt the difficult climb or the descent.

It was easy to communicate on this island as everyone spoke English, and the currency was English Sterling. Being a British outpost, the Union Jack flew proudly there.

Mum and Dad loved their time on this island. It was a perfect day out. Things changed when they got back to their cabin for a shower. They noticed there was a plumbing problem, with no water and an awful sewerage smell. Unable to have a shower, they waited patiently for three hours. Feeling hungry and not wanting to go out without a shower, they ordered sandwiches for tea in their room. It was delivered on a platter with crisps and salad. The water came on, but it was only a trickle. However, they both jumped under for an unfulfilling shower. By the morning the water was back to normal.

Four days later, 12th April, they found a message left in their cabin to get in touch with the ship's purser. They spoke to the purser, and he apologetically asked if they minded changing cabins, as their cabin was requiring maintenance with the overhead plumbing. Accepting this offer, they were given an upgrade to a higher deck cabin that was much bigger, with a porthole and a full-size bathroom. The cabin attendants packed all their clothes and carried them up to the new cabin. The upgrade was well received, even though there were only six more nights on the ship before they reached Southampton.

Mum and Dad noticed they slept in a bit more in this new cabin, finding it a much quieter location on the ship.

Tenerife, Canary Islands

The next port of call was Tenerife, which is the largest island out of the eight Canary Islands, off the coastline of West Africa but belonging to Spain. Mum and Dad enjoyed several hours ashore exploring the port, Santa Cruz.

Funchal Madeira, Portugal

The following morning, Mum and Dad arrived in Funchal Port on Madeira Island. It was a small island in the Atlantic Ocean belonging to Portugal. Here they went ashore to the port town. A lovely photo shows them enjoying a pint of beer, Coral Larger, made locally by The Madeira Brewery that had been operating since 1969. From the photos, I could see the weather was getting much cooler. Mum and Dad were wearing jumpers and long trousers as they travelled into the northern hemisphere in early springtime.

They had two more days at sea before they arrived at their destination, England. It was time to farewell their cruise friends and the staff that had taken great care of them the entire voyage. The staff organised many special parties. There were ice sculptures with elaborate decorations on the banquet tables. Their final night on board, they celebrated in style, going to a formal dinner party. Their waitress, Claire, had been with them the entire cruise and she gave them all the menus from the cruise and wrote a beautiful message of kindness to Mum and Dad.

Southhampton, England - Disembark

Disembarking from the Queen Elizabeth II ship in Southampton would have brought back Dad's memories of his young army days, and now his boots were back on English soil.

He was very proud to have afforded and experienced with Mum such a wonderfully exclusive world cruise. They intended to enjoy catching up with family, friends and their familiar stomping grounds for the next four weeks. Later arriving back in Sydney, Australia on Sunday the 19th of May, 2002.

I always had a strong pull to move to Queensland ever since I left my farm life in Mudgee in 1989. I had even booked a flight in 1990 to move interstate, but no sooner had I got the ticket in my hand, I was offered a full-time office job too good to refuse. I accepted this offer and cancelled my ticket. Ten years later, moving north popped up again. This time it wasn't just me, it was with my husband and our two little boys that were going to be uprooted.

I know where I get my itchy feet from, yes Dad, and the Hinchcliffe lineage. Paul has moved around a lot too, mainly because of his work postings with the bank. John must take after the Pearson lineage, having relaxed and content feet.

After a few trips to Queensland exploring both the Sunshine Coast and the Gold Coast in search of land, we finally settled on acreage at Yandina Creek on the Sunshine Coast. Gary was prepared to commute by car from the Sunshine Coast to Brisbane, then by air to Sydney airport, just to sign onto his work shifts. He was still based out of Sydney, working as an international flight attendant.

John lived locally by himself in a flat in Wollongong, NSW still working at the Pit. Evelyne, Dione, and Claire lived in Fairy Meadow, which was nearby. Paul, Deborah, Peter and Emma were already living in Brisbane, Queensland. Mum and Dad were disappointed about our interstate plans after they had packed up their beautiful home, leaving their beloved English lifestyle behind again.

After we sold our Wollongong house, in early 2003, it was time for a little holiday with Mum and Dad on the Gold Coast. Gary was finalising the interstate move and had work trips to complete, so he stayed back in Wollongong for a few more weeks.

To treat ourselves for our next adventure, we hired a limousine to take us all to the airport. The limousine hires, with three adults and two children, was reasonably priced compared to other airport bus connections. It was George and Harry's first ride in a limousine. The boys had their loud holiday shirts on, along with their cool sunglasses. George was four and Harry two-years-old, both very cute and excited little travellers.

Arriving on the Gold Coast, we stayed in a comfortable two-bedroom apartment near the beach. The boys and I had one week with Mum and Dad, then they stayed on for an extra week's holiday in the apartment by themselves. Deborah drove down from Brisbane to collect the boys and me. We were staying with them in their new home initially, at Mt Gravatt, which they had recently finished building. Three months later, we moved into a rented flat at Peregian Beach, nearer to our land, so we could start building our house.

Despite no practical house building experience between Gary and I, we decided to "owner-build" our house, which was quite a learning curve. Gary did a weekend owner-builder registration course, theory only. From start to finish, it took nine months to complete the house build. During that time, Mum and Dad visited both Paul and me in Queensland for mini holidays from NSW. We moved into our new house on Australia Day long weekend in January 2004.

Our land was steep, so our gardens needed some stone retaining walls. It was Dad's idea to use the dry-stone wall effect that he had grown up with in Yorkshire as a young lad. Many dry walls still exist today in England, Wales and Scotland for dividing farms into separate fields for their livestock.

I collected the stones from our land so he could select the best ones for building our dry-stone retaining walls. Being very proud to be building Yorkshire dry stone walls in Queensland, he took a lot of pleasure in working with the stones, creating many of our beautiful walls.

Both Paul and I were settled in our new houses, happily living in Queensland. John hadn't retired yet, still working in the coal mine.

He had dreams of buying a houseboat to retire on in northern NSW or southern Queensland. Mum and Dad were faced with the difficult decision of where to live again, Queensland versus NSW. Dad was 69-years-old and feeling anxious about not knowing where they would finally settle down and enjoy retirement.

They decided to move up to the Sunshine Coast in Queensland. They packed up all their belongings, again. After their unit was sold, they became homeless until Paul, John and I could buy them an apartment to live in. The search for a home took many months, a much longer process than we had all anticipated. John was having a very difficult year with his health. We all searched for the right property which became challenging with so many people involved in the decision making. Their furniture and belongings all went into storage. During the waiting period my parent's lived between Paul's and my house. Sometimes, they enjoyed short holiday breaks.

Pacific Ocean Cruising (2004)

John recalls Dad was reluctant to spend our inheritance, but knew he needed to have a holiday from all the stress of not knowing where he was going to live. John bought Mum and Dad gifts for their holiday and remembers giving Dad a beautiful brass telescope in a leather case. It was returned to John from Mum, now being a family keepsake.

The travel agent offered Dad the opportunity to do two seven-day Pacific Ocean cruising holidays back-to-back at a very reduced price. They travelled in February to March 2004 from Sydney Harbour around the Pacific Ocean islands, twice. They had a wonderful 14 day holiday.

On one of the island visits, Dad sat chatting to the island chief on the beach, while Mum went on an island tour with other passengers. The island chief suggested to Dad that they move to his island for the perfect lifestyle. Dad said he felt tempted. It was very peaceful and beautiful there. Cruising was a favourite way to travel for them both. To celebrate Mum and Dad's 49th wedding anniversary, Gary and I booked them into a local à-la-carte restaurant near Yandina called The Rocks. The restaurant was nestled on the banks of the winding Maroochy River, set among rolling hills of farming pastures. overlooking the peaceful river.

Paul, Alison, John (children), Claire, Dione, George, Emma, Harry, Peter (grandchildren).

"Which beauty spot is this dear", faxed drawing by Arnold, inspired from their coast to coast walk.

QE2 formal dinner attire.

QE2 port of call, Tenerife, Canary Islands.

Alison Simpson

12
UNPACKING FOR GOOD

River Views

Paul, John and I went thirds in buying a large three-bedroom unit on Bradman Avenue Maroochydore, for Mum and Dad. It had stunning views facing north on the Maroochy River. They moved into their new home in late October (2004) and quickly got to work unpacking their boxes and setting up the spacious unit into a very comfortable home. Within a week, they had unpacked everything and could finally relax.

I picked up the boys from school in the afternoon and drove straight to their new unit. We had organised a little family party for George's fifth birthday, on the 2nd of November. Mum and Dad had set up their new wooden outdoor table and chairs on the balcony with lovely party food and gifts for the boys.

We sat on the expansive balcony enjoying the space and the gorgeous river view. It was a lovely home for them. There were sailing boats, jet skiers, fishermen, cyclists and walkers to watch every day, a constantly changing vista of river enthusiasts. Dad bought a few plant pots and soon filled them with flowers and herbs, happy to have some space to continue his gardening joy.

Dad suggested to Mum that they go to the Wednesday Eumundi Markets for a nice day out on the 17th of November. They caught a bus from Bradman Avenue then changed buses at Nambour, to get a second bus to Eumundi township. Mum felt it was a nice day out at the markets however, she noticed that Dad didn't have a lot of energy and needed to stop often to sit down and rest.

At breakfast on the morning of the 18th of November, Mum and Dad were discussing the idea of buying themselves a bicycle each for Christmas, which was only five weeks away. Their unit was in good proximity to cycle ways and footpaths for cycling along the flat terrain into Maroochydore, following the coastline beaches to Mooloolaba.

After breakfast, Dad didn't feel well. He had a sore throat and felt very tired. He went to lie down on his bed. Following a short rest, he came back looking for some Lemsip and to make a cup of tea, asking Mum if she wanted a cuppa too. He put the kettle on, turned to face Mum, then fell directly onto the floor with a fatal heart attack.

Mum turned around to talk to him and he had disappeared onto the floor behind the kitchen breakfast bar. She said he fell silently. It happened so quickly, seemingly out of the blue. Mum called 000 for an ambulance and applied CPR until the ambulance paramedics arrived. I then received the distressed call from Mum.

When I woke up that morning, I dropped George off at school and my intuition told me to drop Harry into day-care, not being his usual day. Thankfully, they had a spare place for him. Next, I had to decide where would I do the weekly grocery shopping. I only had two options, either Maroochydore or Noosa, both being a good 25-minute drive in opposite directions. Thankfully, I opted for Maroochydore and was driving in that direction when I felt a sharp lightning bolt of pain through my chest. Within moments of that pain, I had a phone call. I pulled over onto the side of the road and Mum gave me the saddest news that Dad had a fatal heart attack. I was about 15 minutes away from their unit.

As I drove up to the unit, the ambulance was in the driveway. When I looked up onto their balcony, I saw Mum sitting in a chair facing the river with a man standing behind her. He had his hands on her shoulders, looking down at her. I felt it was Dad, because the paramedic was in the apartment.

I parked the car and ran up the stairs. As I opened the front door, I saw Dad's body on the kitchen floor. I gently stepped around his lifeless body and went straight outside to see Mum on the balcony. I gave her a big hug, and we both cried. I dispiritedly phoned Paul so he could then contact John.

For many years later, an ambulance siren would always trigger my memory of that time. Not a day goes past when I don't think of my dad. Life has been quite difficult for Mum since he passed. Dad was the one who managed most things. He had taken great care of Mum during their life together. She was "the apple of his eye" to cherish above all others. What an amazing 70 years Dad, until we meet again. xxx

Alison Simpson

EPILOGUE

Family Reflections

Paul instantly became the Hinchcliffe tribe leader. He was able to calmly organise Dad's funeral, the rest of us had no hope of attending to the fine details or even knowing where to start. For me, that time was simply a blur. Paul contacted the Grenadier Guard Association with Dad's funeral details. We were incredibly blessed to have two retired Guards attend Dad's formal funeral service in Brisbane. That was very special for our family, as we knew how much he was proud of being a Guardsman.

Years later, Paul moved into a new home on Mount Tamborine Mountain, with beautiful views overlooking the skyline of Surfers Paradise. Paul has since retired but still works many hours voluntarily for the State Emergency Services and loves his long-distance trekking adventures. Paul completed the entire Coast to Coast Walk across England, twice. He walked from the Irish Sea in the West to the North Sea in the East in both 2012 and 2014. On his second walk, in 2014, he dropped pebbles along the way with Dad's name on them, in memory of our Dad. I'm sure Dad would have taken every step alongside Paul from St Bees in the west to Robin Hood Bay in the east, in spirit.

John finished 27 years of coal mining in March 2005 due to ill health. In April, he moved in with Mum for a few short months to support her after she had a hip replacement. In 2011, John bought his dream houseboat in dock on Hope Island, Gold Coast, Queensland. John had suffered two strokes in both 2012 and 2013. He was unable to live independently so he sold his houseboat and moved into a nursing home on the Gold Coast.

After a third major stroke, very sadly, John passed away on his birthday, the 27th of November 2021, aged 64 years. Paul oversaw John's care for the entire time he lived in the nursing home of eight years. He regularly took John out for lunch, shopping, and they often went to the movies together. John had built quite a reputation at the nursing home for lightening up the atmosphere with his wicked sense of humour. He always saw the funny side of life.

John was the closest to Dad throughout life, especially after working alongside him in the Pit. I could see my Grandad, Stanley Hinchcliffe, in John's face in his final days.

Mum found life unbearable without Dad. He was the one who organised most things, including all the family finances. She dropped in and out of deep sadness many times. Her sister, Joy and partner, Don, came over from England to support her for as long as they could. Mum was very grateful for their time.

In 2006, Mum had a stroke, but recovered quite well and was able to care for herself independently. I was with her having breakfast when I noticed her face drooping, unable to eat. She had a second stroke in the car as I drove her to hospital. A couple of months later she took herself to England for a holiday to see her sisters. Mum now lives in an Over 50s Retirement Village just off Bradman Avenue, near Maroochy River and enjoys walking along the river. I'm able to look out for her living only a 15-minute drive away. We go shopping every Friday, enjoying our day out together. Mum loves writing emails to her sister Joy and handwritten letters to her two other sisters, Barbara and Mary, of whom all live in England. She loves doing word puzzles, scrabble and reading. Mum loves a social whisky and dry ginger.

Mum had a psychic reading with a clairvoyant when she was young. The life prediction for her was that she would have "many keys". She was hoping it meant typewriter keys, perhaps becoming a stenographer (secretary). No, it was house keys. In her entire marriage from 1955 to 2004, they had owned 26 front door keys from all their moving around. She has since slowed down, only having three keys from 2004. After Dad's passing, her favourite house key was when she came with my young family to England for our working holiday of two years in 2009 and 2010. We lived in Caversham, Reading, England. Mum loved catching a train into London, then a second train to Dover, to visit her sisters. I'm sure Dad was by her side on those trips. We all have cherished memories of that happy time living in England.

My family moved from our small acreage to suburbia, to be closer to the beach in 2015. The boys are young adults and still live at home with us in 2022. Gary has retired recently and I'm self-employed. I love working in the field of natural medicine, fitness and wellbeing. My favourite pastimes are going to the beach, travelling, gardening and, most importantly, writing. There are many more books in me as I plan on living a very long life.

I'm so grateful Dad started his life story with Paul, so I could complete it for him. I have learnt so much more about him as I researched his life. Dad was a hard worker and always strived to support his family first. He was a kind and loving father. I don't ever remember him raising his voice or getting angry at me. He was a gentle soul. All his beautiful hand writings signed off "God Bless". Never going to church, he was still a deep thinker with his own understanding of spirituality. He taught his children well through heartfelt actions rather than words.

The apple never falls far from the tree.

*Arnold in his retired serviceman uniform;
The Grenadier Guard Association blazer and tie.*

"Ee Bah Gum" The Yorkshireman

www.ingramcontent.com/pod-product-compliance
Lightning Source LLC
Chambersburg PA
CBHW051430290426
44109CB00016B/1500